REBELLION IN CHIAPAS

TRANSFORMATION OF RURAL MEXICO SERIES, Number 5
EJIDO REFORM RESEARCH PROJECT
CENTER FOR U.S.-MEXICAN STUDIES
UNIVERSITY OF CALIFORNIA, SAN DIEGO

David Myhre, Series Editor

PRINTED WITH THE ASSISTANCE
OF THE FORD FOUNDATION

REBELLION IN CHIAPAS:
RURAL REFORMS, CAMPESINO RADICALISM, AND THE LIMITS TO SALINISMO
revised and updated

by

NEIL HARVEY

---

with additional essays

THE CHIAPAS UPRISING

by

LUIS HERNÁNDEZ NAVARRO

and

INDIGENOUS AUTONOMY AND POWER IN CHIAPAS: LESSONS FROM MOBILIZATION IN JUCHITÁN

by

JEFFREY W. RUBIN

TRANSFORMATION OF RURAL MEXICO, Number 5
EJIDO REFORM RESEARCH PROJECT
CENTER FOR U.S.-MEXICAN STUDIES, UCSD

Printed in the United States of America by
the Center for U.S.-Mexican Studies
University of California, San Diego

1994

Cover: Linoleum block print by Annika Nelson

ISBN 1-878367-23-4

Suggested Citation Style for Individual Essays
Cite by individual author and title, as in the following example:

Harvey, Neil. 1994. "Rebellion in Chiapas: Rural Reforms, Campesino Radicalism, and the Limits to Salinismo" (revised and updated). Pp. 1-49 in *TheTransformation of Rural Mexico,* Number 5 (La Jolla, California: Center for U.S.-Mexican Studies, University of California at San Diego).

NB: The information and analysis presented herein are the responsibility of the author of each essay.

TABLE OF CONTENTS

MAP OF CHIAPAS

Major Regions

1 Centro	4 Frailesca	7 Sierra
2 Altos	5 Norte	8 Soconusco
3 Fronteriza	6 Selva	9 Costa

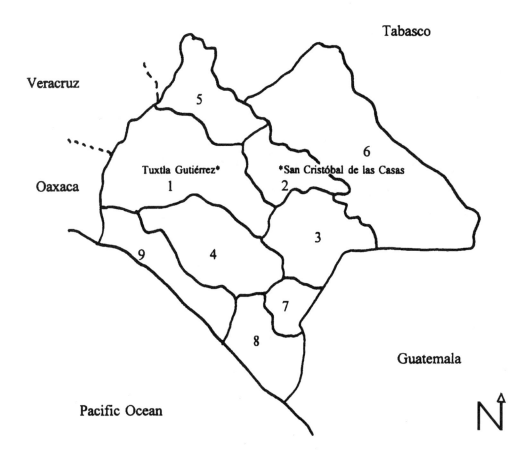

REBELLION IN CHIAPAS:
RURAL REFORMS, CAMPESINO RADICALISM, AND THE LIMITS TO SALINISMO[1]

by

NEIL HARVEY[2]

The armed uprising by between three and four thousand Indians in Chiapas on January 1, 1994 took virtually everyone by surprise. Even people familiar with the region were astonished by the scale of the rebellion and the remarkably sophisticated organization which had evidently been prepared over several years. The tactics of the Ejército Zapatista de Liberación Nacional (EZLN) differed from the *foco* strategies of earlier guerrilla movements in Mexico and Latin America. Unlike its precursors, the EZLN is not a small band of rebels hoping to attract support by rising up in arms. This movement already had its a mass base when it made its appearance.

The origins and significance of the uprising have been debated by many analysts and it clearly represents a watershed in modern Mexican history. This paper discusses its rural dimension. It attempts to show how policies to modernize the economy and a series of rural reforms have had a negative impact for most campesinos in Chiapas, particularly in the Selva and Altos regions.

The rebellion is unlike previous guerrilla struggles in Latin America in that it does not aspire by itself to seize state power and lead the masses in social revolution. In its declaration of war on the federal army and government, the Zapatistas called on all Mexicans to participate in whatever way they can, not necessarily with arms, in a broad movement for "jobs, land, housing, food, health,

1. Revised, with an update reviewing and analyzing events from February to September, 1994.

2. Communications may be sent to the author at the Department of Government, New Mexico State University, Box 30001/Dept. 3BN, Las Cruces, NM 88003-0001, USA. Tel:(505) 646-4935 and 646-3220; Fax: (505) 646-3725; e-mail: nharvey@nmsu.edu

I would like to thank David Myhre, coordinator of the Ejido Reform Research Project at the Center for U.S.-Mexican Studies, University of California at San Diego, for his encouragement and assistance in the writing of this paper. Financial support for field work in 1991-92 was provided by the Economic and Social Research Council (UK), award number R232486. Funding for field work in January 1993, January 1994 and in July-August 1994 was provided by a grant made available through the Instituto de Investigaciones Sociales (IIS) at the Universidad Nacional Autónoma de México (UNAM). Additional funding for the 1994 field work was provided by the Ejido Reform Research Project.

I would also like to thank the director of the IIS, Dr. Ricardo Pozas Horcasitas, and Dr. Humberto Carton de Grammont for their invaluable support for my research in Mexico. I also acknowledge the great generosity shown by many people during the course of my research on Chiapas, including my mother, Sheila Price, Bob Curtis, Joe Foweraker, Eduardo Ontiveros, María Elena Ontiveros, María Eugenia Reyes Ramos, Walda Barrios, Antonio Mosquera, Juan Balboa, Frida Quiroga and Pancho Gómez. Finally I thank my wife Wendy for her constant support and love, and particularly for her help in the writing of this paper.

education, independence, freedom, democracy, justice and peace." Its political discourse is therefore extremely modern in comparison to Sendero Luminoso and earlier guerrilla organizations. Rather than engage in a "war of movement" to destroy the state, the EZLN represents more of a "war of position" aimed at shifting the balance of forces in favor of popular and democratic movements, thereby isolating and ultimately defeating anti-democratic tendencies within the ruling Partido Revolucionario Institucional (PRI), the state and the rest of society (Gramsci 1971).

Its stated political objectives are to make government accountable to the people and to achieve effective representation for all Mexicans, particularly the indigenous population. It justified the uprising in terms of the lack of conditions for free and democratic elections, calling on the legislative and judicial branches of government to depose the president, Carlos Salinas de Gortari, and install a transitional government to organize fair elections. The rebellion was also directed against the economic model implemented by Salinas. The seizure of seven towns on January 1, 1994 was timed to coincide with the entry into effect of the North American Free Trade Agreement (NAFTA). One of the first EZLN communiques stated that NAFTA "is a death certificate for the Indian peoples of Mexico, who are dispensable for the government of Carlos Salinas de Gortari". The EZLN also called for the redistribution of *latifundios* (large private estates) and the repeal of reforms carried out in 1992 to Article 27 of the Constitution (the statutes governing land tenure).

This paper characterizes the uprising as a rural rebellion. This does not mean that its impact is limited to rural problems, far removed from the concerns of urban people. On the contrary, throughout Mexican history campesinos have played a crucial role in national political crises. Despite this protagonism their interests and cultures are usually subordinated to the new political and economic elites which emerge from these crises. Will it be the same story this time round? Will the much heralded political reform lead to the type of changes which are being demanded by the Indians of Chiapas? Or will it simply reimpose the same sort of biases against the rural poor and continue to foreclose alternative paths of development for indigenous peoples? In short, what types of changes are necessary if the rural dimension is not to be forgotten?

In order to approach these questions the paper is divided into four main sections. The first locates the Chiapas uprising in its historical context. It is seen as a response to the restructuring of capital on a global scale and as a continuation of previous rural rebellions in defense of economic and political rights. As such it reveals the crisis of legitimation for the Mexican state in rural areas, much as earlier rebellions have done.

The second discusses the effects of agricultural modernization and institutional reforms in Chiapas. It begins by emphasizing the constraints faced by the social sector and, by way of contrast, notes the expansion of private sector commercial agriculture after 1982.[3] Attention is then given to

---

3. The social sector in rural Mexico refers to lands which were redistributed under the agrarian reform program mandated by Article 27 after the 1910-17 Revolution. These sector is comprised of *ejidos* and *comunidades agrarias,* comprised of *ejidatarios* and *comuneros*, respectively. The former refer to lands which the state redistributed through the break up of private holdings or through the colonization of unused "national lands". The latter refers to lands historically held by indigenous communities, as well as to communities established through petitions to recuperate areas lost to encroachment by private owners.

the effects of institutional reforms in the coffee and maize sectors. The Salinas government's Solidaridad program is then examined in the light of the problems facing the social sector in Chiapas.

The third section discusses the effects of the modifications to land tenure and agrarian codes which were approved by Congress in December, 1991 and February, 1992 - a process widely known as "ejido reform." It describes the recent history of limited land distribution in Chiapas and the repression suffered by legal campesino organizations. This contributed to the generally negative reception of the ejido reform, particularly in the Selva region. The content and implications for Chiapas of the changes to Article 27 are discussed with this backdrop in mind. Although the measurable, direct effects of the ejido reform may not be seen for many years, the effects on campesino expectations have had no greater expression than the rebellion itself. In particular the legislated end of land reform was interpreted as the final break in the government's commitment to the rural poor. The loss of hope in acceding to a piece of land contributed to the radicalization of thousands of Indians in eastern Chiapas.

The fourth section describes the process of campesino organizing in the Selva since the early 1970s, with the goal of explaining why the EZLN was able to attract support in this particular region. The failure of successive governments to provide economic support and political space for representative campesino organizations is seen to have contributed to a weakening of legalistic strategies and the radicalization of discontent. These findings differ from the argument put forward by Warman (1994) who claims that the rebellion was implanted from outside by political activists pursuing their own agenda. The analysis presented here is closer to that of Hernández (1994) and local campesino leaders. One of the interviews given by the EZLN _subcomandante_ Marcos also reveals the desperation caused by the authorities' constant rejection of popular demands and proposals (_La Jornada_, 6 February 1994).

The paper concludes by reflecting on the limits to _salinismo_ in rural Mexico and the need to incorporate alternative strategies for rural development through the democratization of rural power relations.

I. CHIAPAS AND THE CRISIS OF LEGITIMATION IN RURAL MEXICO

The rebellion in Chiapas is a response of indigenous peoples to economic changes which threaten their main source of livelihood: access to land. These changes are not unique to Mexico but are part of the restructuring of capital on a global scale and the differential insertion of agricultural activities in the international political economy (McMichael and Myhre 1991). Under capitalism the

---

communities, as well as to communities established through petitions to recuperate areas lost to encroachment by private owners.

continuous search for profits creates and reproduces the demand for new and more lucrative commodities among the wealthier classes. As Marx predicted, the expansion of capitalism and commercial agriculture were generally made at the expense of peasant societies.

In the post-war period the modernization of agriculture in developing countries was supported by international research foundations and national governments through the application of Green Revolution technology. Global food output boomed but the problems of rural poverty and hunger did not disappear. Policy was biased in favor of urban consumers and the needs of rapid industrialization. As rural producers became increasingly differentiated, competition for land, water and inputs increased. Export crops expanded, drawing in former subsistence producers into new global markets. The recession in the industrialized countries in the early 1980s reduced demand and world commodity prices began to fall. At the same time Latin American countries were burdened by the debt crisis and generally responded by cutting public expenditure and restructuring their economies to allow a central role for private capital. In this context transnational capital and multilateral lending institutions were able to influence the policy decisions of national governments. Privatization of state enterprises, the elimination of subsidies and the opening of domestic markets to cheaper imports were adopted throughout Latin America. Only those producers with sufficient capital, land and technology to compete in the world market became viable.

Some smaller producers were able to gain access to niche markets or sought ways to associate with private investors. However, the majority of rural producers found themselves occupying a more marginal role in the new economy. A new rural underclass has been emerging throughout Latin America, made up particularly of young people with little prospects for economic improvement. The rapid increase in migration is one indication of this. Another is the political organization of rural movements seeking to defend small farmers and redefine their insertion into the market on more advantageous terms. Both of these types of responses have been widespread in Mexico, especially since 1982. The third option, one which has always existed in the Latin American context, is the one taken by the *Zapatistas* of Chiapas.

The subordination of campesinos to capital varied in accordance with local historical and cultural factors. As a result, economic relations were always mediated by political struggle. In Mexico there is a long history of rural rebellion which has shaped the relationship between capital, campesinos and the state.

The direct causes for revolt have been many (Katz 1988). In the colonial period the most important were the exaction of tribute and taxes and threats to local autonomy and religious practices. In Chiapas, the 1712 Tzeltal rebellion was provoked by the Church's efforts to extract ever larger tithes from indigenous communities and destroy native religious beliefs and practices. In the nineteenth and early twentieth centuries it was the loss of land and water rights which led to rebellion. In highland Chiapas the loss of community lands and the reduction to peon status with few rights led thousands of Indians to declare war on non-Indians in the Caste War of 1868-70. In post-revolutionary Mexico the main causes of rural unrest have been associated with the abandonment of the land reform and campesino agriculture after 1938. In the 1970s land invasions occurred in many states as campesinos tired of waiting for the implementation of titles in their favor. In the

1980s the focus of rural movements shifted to contest the decline in state subsidies and support for the reform sector. In Chiapas land conflicts continued to be the main source of unrest until the 1990s.

If we adopt an historical perspective, two main factors appear as central to explaining the occurrence of rural rebellion in Mexico. The first of these concerns the impact of institutional reforms to support a new cycle of capital accumulation. The second is the weakness of the state in rural areas. The Bourbon reforms of the late eighteenth century and the privatization of community lands under the dictatorship of Porfirio Díaz one hundred years later provoked widespread rural rebellions which, unique in the Latin American context, fed into national revolutions (Coatsworth 1988). On the other hand, the desire of the colonial governments to constrain the power of creole elites led it to uphold the demands of indigenous communities in defending land and autonomy. With independence, however, the Mexican state did not exist as such and national governments tended to be the military allies of regional landowning elites. There was no attempt to support the Indians or non-Indian campesinos, leading to the rise in rebelliousness in 1840-70. Defeat in external war and foreign intervention also weakened the state, allowing for various alliances between campesinos and local leaders.

Although the number of rebellions declined under the Díaz dictatorship, this was due more to fear of repression than any effective mediating of land disputes. The _porfirista_ state was not strong, it was personalistic and fell when Díaz went into exile. The formation of the post-revolutionary state was based on the defeat of rural social movements, symbolized by the assassination of Emiliano Zapata in 1919. The ruling party attempted to coopt the image of Zapata into its agrarian discourse but for many the ideals of _zapatismo_ could live on only through independent organization and struggle. The importance of Zapata in campesino consciousness was reasserted in the wake of new agrarian movements in the 1970s and early 1980s (Flores Lúa, Paré and Sarmiento 1988).

Since 1917 the basis of political legitimation for the Mexican state was the revolutionary Constitution and its specific measures in favor of the rights of workers and campesinos. During the next six decades various expressions of state intervention in the rural economy created new channels and strategies for linking the state to every aspect of rural life. Of all of these, land reform remained the central pillar of stability. For those campesinos who could not be given land, the state even created a mechanism to at least assure their acquiescence: the _ejidatario con derechos a salvo_ was promised a piece of land at some future date when further redistribution allowed. Agrarian populism was given a new boost by the reforms of Echeverría in 1970-76, leading to the celebrated expropriation of prime irrigated land in Sonora for redistribution among campesino groups. The explosion of governmental agencies in this period established new linkages and sources of political legitimation, and corruption, for the state. Thanks to the oil-debt boom, the sudden policy shift towards support for campesino grain producers in 1980-82 added a new set of institutions and bolstered others, particularly in the areas of grain purchasing and food supply in southern Mexico (Fox 1992).

None of these interventions secured total hegemony, in the Gramscian sense. The institutional bases for legitimation tended to be weaker the further one went from Mexico City. Everyday forms of resistance and oppositional "hidden transcripts" of the type described by Scott (1985, 1990) undoubtedly lay behind public deference to the bureaucrats and *licenciados*. The expansion of the state also created spaces for resistance as campesinos sought favor with one agency director in their battles with another or in their conflicts with landowners. Legitimation was more of a strategy than a complete edifice, but what is significant about the period from 1940 through 1982 is that the state could create so many mechanisms and strategies to assure, at a national level, relative rural peace.

The economic reforms of the post-crisis period have thus had an impact at two levels. On the one hand, as Alan Knight (1993) calls it, the new Bourbon project of the technocrats is designed to create the conditions for a new cycle of capital accumulation. But, on the other, it proceeds by eroding previous sources of legitimation. The regime's central dilemma has therefore been how to construct new bases of support for a project which, at least in the short-term, demands austerity and sacrifice in the hope of future benefits (Harvey 1993). In the urban sector the dilemma is partially resolved by controlling inflation and opening the borders to consumer imports. The return of capital provides for new investment and jobs and legitimation becomes a function of economic performance. In the countryside, however, investment is nowhere to be seen. Infrastructure lies idle. Credit has dried up for all but a few and markets are saturated with imported grains. In this context the rural reforms since 1982 weakened earlier sources of legitimation without providing new channels capable of mediating popular demands.

The rebellion in Chiapas, like its antecedents, revealed a crisis of legitimation for the state in rural Mexico. It can be understood by referring to the limits to *salinismo*, the political discourse associated with the administration of Carlos Salinas de Gortari. The defining elements of *salinismo* were economic liberalization, institutional reform of the state and targeted social programs. For many campesinos in Chiapas and other regions these have meant increasing exclusion from markets, abandonment by the state and the political manipulation of limited social spending.

II. MODERNIZATION AND INSTITUTIONAL REFORMS

The Rural Social Sector in Chiapas

Any analysis of the implications of the rural reforms for campesino agriculture must begin with an understanding of the conditions of the social sector. Table 1 provides a general panorama for the state of Chiapas, using official data from 1988 (INEGI 1991). From this data we can gain a picture of the relatively poor level of development of ejidos and comunidades agrarias in Chiapas. Virtually all of the sector is dedicated to rainfed agriculture. If we calculate that each of the almost 200,000 ejidatarios or comuneros has five or six dependents, the population we are referring to is over one million persons, occupying a little over 3 million hectares of land,[4] of which only 40.8 percent is classified as good for agricultural use. Maize is clearly the principal crop for most ejidos and comunidades agrarias, followed by coffee. However, the figures do not indicate the combination of crops within each ejido. Survey data for 1990 also revealed that 44.6 percent of ejidatarios possessed between 0.1 and 4.0 hectares and 42.0 percent had plots between 4.1 and 10.0 hectares (SARH-CEPAL 1992, p.3). In the Altos region, the average plot size is 2 hectares.

In terms of opportunities to convert to new cash crops, it should be noted that the sixteen ejidos which produced soy beans were all located in the more developed Soconusco region. Ten percent of ejidos in the Soconusco also had access to irrigation. Regarding the limited use of inputs, we can add that the category of "public services" tends to present a somewhat distorted picture of reality. This rubric includes electricity, drinking water, paved and unpaved roads. The fact that three quarters of the ejidos reported that they had unpaved roads (1,224) hardly constitutes access to public services. A more accurate indication is given by the low proportion which had paved roads (10 percent). Installation of electricity and drinking water was said to benefit 50 and 35 percent of ejidos, respectively.

According to the 1988 survey 62.5 percent of the rural social sector in Mexico received credit in 1988. In Chiapas the figure was given at 55.5 percent. The regions with the lowest proportion of credit were the Altos and Selva (30 and 38 percent, respectively). However, the validity of these figures is contradicted by other sources. More recent data show that, at a national level, during the period 1985-89 only 22.2 percent of ejidatarios and comuneros had access to credit each year, falling to 16.3 percent in 1990. In fact, between 1985 and 1990 62 percent of producers in the social sector had no access whatsoever to agricultural credit (SARH-CEPAL 1992, p.19).[5] In Chiapas the number of producers with credit for planting fell from an annual average of 20.4 percent in 1985-89 to 12.7 in 1990, while only 5.7 percent of producers received credit for machinery in 1985-90. Similarly, the Confederación Nacional Campesina (CNC) claimed that, in 1987 only 43 percent of ejidos in Mexico received credit (Equipo Pueblo/Instituto Maya 1988, p.49). Moreover, the INEGI survey gives us no indication of the amount of credit each ejido or comunidad agraria were said to have received.

At the same time that productivity of basic grains was declining, the growth of private sector commercial agriculture boomed in Chiapas. Although starting from a lower base, between 1982 and 1987 the land area dedicated to new cash crops of soy beans, peanuts, sorghum and tobacco grew by 51.4, 64.5, 146.8 and 194.9 percent, respectively. Production of these four crops grew by 150.8, 244.1, 144.8 and 261.2 percent in the same period. The more traditional export crops also continued

---

4. One hectare is the equivalent of 2.47 acres.

5. This survey was part of a joint SARH-CEPAL project to construct a typology of producers in the social sector. An earlier typology published in 1982 relies on data from 1970, hence the need for more recent information. See CEPAL 1982; SARH-CEPAL 1992. Note that credit for purchasing or repairing machinery was particularly scarce. Only 10 percent of producers could obtain this type of financing between 1985 and 1990.

Table 1

THE SOCIAL SECTOR IN CHIAPAS IN 1988

Number of ejidos and comunidades agrarias (CA)	1,714
Number of ejidatarios and comuneros	193,515
Land surface in social sector (hectares)	3,130,892
Share of total land area in Chiapas	41.4%

Land use in the social sector	hectares	% of sector
-agriculture	1,278,147	40.8
-forestry	700,381	22.4
-pasture	923,182	29.5
-other uses	229,182	7.3
-rainfed area	1,225,831	95.9
-irrigated area	52,316	4.1

Principal crop cultivated	No. of Ejidos & CA
-maize	1,264
-coffee	349
-sugar cane	19
-soy beans	16
-beans	8
-green vegetables	8
-rice	3

Inputs in the social sector	No. of Ejidos & CA	% of sector
-farm installations	495	28.9
-tractors	318	18.6
-agroindustry equipment	206	12.0
-credit	951	55.5
-public services	1,390	81.1

Source: INEGI 1991.

NB: The number of ejidos and comunidades agrarias in Chiapas increased by
    358 in 1989-92, to 2,072 (PROCEDE 1993, p.10).

to expand. Banana production increased by over 25 percent, while output of cacao and sugar cane doubled. In 1982-87 the volume of meat production also increased by over 400 percent, reflecting the support which ranchers found in the state government (Thompson González, García Aguilar and Castillo Huerta 1988, pp.225-30).

The modernization policies were continued by governor Patrocinio González Garrido (1989-93). In 1989 his government ordered the privatization of two state-owned enterprises, the Chiapas Forestry Corporation (CORFO) and the Pujiltic sugar mill.[6] The *Plan de Gobierno 1989-94* was also designed to promote export agriculture through improvements to port facilities at Puerto Madero and continued support for producers of sorghum, peanuts, soy beans, and safflower. The most significant reforms of this period, however, concerned the two main crops produced by campesinos in Chiapas: coffee and maize.

Restructuring the Coffee Sector

For many years small coffee growers sold their crop to a state agency, the Instituto Nacional Mexicano del Café (INMECAFE). INMECAFE was established in 1958 to carry out research and provide technical support. As part of Echeverría's strategy to modernize small-scale production and increase the state's presence in regional markets, the functions of INMECAFE were expanded in 1973. It was given a central role in organizing and financing coffee production, as well as guaranteeing the purchase and export of the harvest. By the end of the 1970s it had managed to displace several important intermediaries and purchased half of domestic supply. In Chiapas, this conjuncture allowed for the emergence of new producer co-operatives and Uniones de Ejidos (UE) in both the Altos and Selva regions.

With the economic crisis of the 1980s the position of INMECAFE declined. Its share of the market fell from 44 percent in 1982-83 to just 9.6 percent in 1987-88 (Hernández 1991, p.62). Like many of the state agencies in this period, it suffered from internal inefficiencies, corruption and mismanagement. By 1988 INMECAFE had an accumulated debt of approximately US$90 million.

The response of the Salinas government in 1989 was to begin the process of privatization. INMECAFE immediately withdrew from purchasing and marketing and reduced its provision of technical assistance. Although the reform was originally designed to include the producer organizations in the transfer of infrastructure, the plan lacked the necessary political will and much of the infrastructure lay idle or passed into private ownership.

In 1988 there were 194,000 coffee growers in Mexico, cultivating over 560,000 hectares in twelve states. The skewed nature of production units in this sector is well-known. 71.3 percent of

---

6. The mill was sold for approximately US$14 million (42,000 million old pesos) to the Empresa Operadora Grijalva, a company that processes coffee and sugar. The Pujiltic sale caused discontent among the cane growers who had been arguing for the transfer of the mill to their ownership.

growers have plots of less than two hectares. Another 20.6 percent have areas of between two and five hectares, while just 2 percent have over 10 hectares (Hernández 1991, p.52).

Chiapas, Mexico's principal coffee producing state, presents a similar pattern. Here 73,742 growers occupy 228,264 hectares of land. 91 percent of producers have less than 5 hectares, while 116 private owners possess 12 percent of the area under coffee cultivation (Table 2). In the Selva region, of the almost 17,000 producers, 93 percent have plots of less than two hectares (Hernández 1994).

In June 1989 the International Coffee Organization failed to agree on production quotas, causing the world price to fall by 50 percent. In the ensuing period the Mexican government did not support efforts by other Latin American countries to reestablish a quota system and increase the price paid to producers. Another consequence of Salinas's macroeconomic reforms which hurt coffee producers was the overvalued peso. Potential export earnings which might have offset lower world prices were lost as a result. Between December 1987 and December 1993 domestic inflation increased by 89.3 percent while the exchange rate increased by under 50 percent. As a result, the cost of inputs rose faster than the principal source of income. In addition, in the absence of INMECAFE, marketing costs had to be absorbed by the producers themselves, or alternatively through the reappearance of unregulated private intermediaries, known as "coyotes" (Hernández 1994).

Table 2

**DISTRIBUTION OF COFFEE PRODUCERS BY PLOT SIZE
CHIAPAS AND MEXICO**

Plot size (hectares)	Chiapas	Mexico
up to 2	48,762	194,538
2-5	18,248	64,377
5-10	5,102	17,881
10-20	1,202	4,291
20-50	208	808
50-100	104	246
over 100	116	178
Total	73,742	282,319

Source: INMECAFE 1992.

Following the 1989 crisis it took over three years of negotiations and mobilizations by producer groups before the government agreed to an emergency support program. With less income and the simultaneous reduction of credit, thousands of growers were unable to invest in their crop. Both productivity and total output in the social sector fell by around 35 percent between 1989 and 1993. On average, small producers suffered a 70 percent drop in income in the same period (*La Jornada*, 23 January 1994, p.47). Most producers were caught in a cycle of debt and poverty. Unable to repay loans due to the fall in prices and income, they became ineligible for new loans. The accumulation of debts in this sector reached approximately US$270 million by the end of 1993. In these conditions thousands of small growers in Chiapas abandoned production in 1989-93.

Basic Grains and Trade Liberalization

Another of the institutional reforms concerned the restructuring of state intervention in support of basic grain production and marketing. As with coffee, Chiapas is Mexico's largest maize producing state. The reform process began with the onset of the debt crisis in 1982. Under the administration of Miguel de la Madrid, governmental subsidies to the agricultural sector decreased on average by 13 percent annually, after having increased by 12.5 percent per year during the 1970s. Maize producers faced higher input costs and declining access to credit. By 1987 Banrural provided credit for only 37 percent of the area under maize cultivation and 43 percent in the case of beans. In contrast it financed 52 percent of the land area dedicated to soy beans and 49 percent of sorghum cultivation (Robles 1988). Peso devaluation made inputs more costly, but producers were partly protected by the guaranteed prices which more or less increased in line with inflation in 1983-86 (Hewitt de Alcántara 1992, p.10-12).

This situation began to deteriorate with the signing of the Pacto para la Estabilidad y el Crecimiento Económico (PECE) in December 1987.[7] The Pacto was primarily designed to control inflation which reached almost 200 percent in 1987. The various renewals of the Pacto have been aimed at controlling wages and prices, as well as limiting further devaluation of the peso. Although inflation was brought down to under 20 percent by 1991, the agricultural sector suffered disproportionately. The real value of guaranteed maize prices fell behind the rate of increase in input costs. As a result, the proportion of maize producers operating at a loss jumped from 43 percent in 1987 to 65 percent in 1988 (Hewitt de Alcántara 1992, p.13).

In Chiapas, the withdrawal of state support had a negative effect not only on output and productivity but also on the environment. In the Selva region many campesinos, unable to capitalize their production, continued to clear forested land for subsistence needs. Tropical soils are notoriously unsuited for sustainable agriculture once the biomass has been destroyed. The land may be good for just three or four crops before it is turned into pasture for grazing and the process of deforestation begins anew. Thus, although the land area in Chiapas dedicated to maize increased by 20.6 percent between 1982 and 1987 (from 600,374 to 795,053 hectares), output of this crop in the same period

---

7. The PECE originally was named the Pacto de Solidaridad Económica.

fell by 19.6 percent (from 1.5 million to 1.25 million tons[8]). The same trend was observed for beans. Land area increased by 10 percent but output dropped by 18 percent. Coffee displayed a slight increase in output but this is probably explained by the performance of the large plantations (Thompson González, García Aguilar and Castillo Huerta 1988, pp.225-30).

The Salinas administration accelerated these trends with a series of institutional reforms in 1989. These reforms were also closely related to the World Bank's prescriptions for Mexican agriculture. The Bank conditioned the disbursement of new structural adjustment loans to a radical overhaul of the agricultural sector, recommending the privatization of state-owned enterprises and the gradual elimination of price supports and other input subsidies (McMichael and Myhre 1991; Robles and Moguel 1990).

On the positive side the reforms dealt a blow to corrupt functionaries and inefficient operating procedures. The new discourse of consensus-building, or *concertación*, was initially welcomed by campesino organizations who had been complaining about bureaucratic delays and political manipulation for many years. However, the reforms were not accompanied by the type of financial and marketing support required to reactivate the rural economy. Instead, in most cases, they appeared simply as a means to abandon small-scale producers, all within the discourse of shared responsibilities and *concertación*.[9] As a result, although campesinos were generally glad to see the disappearance in 1989 of the notoriously corrupt Aseguradora Nacional Agrícola y Ganadera (ANAGSA), it also left many without crop insurance. In the same year the Banco Nacional de Crédito Rural (Banrural) stopped all lending to producers in default. This decision particularly affected those maize producers who until the Pacto had managed to maintain productivity levels of the previous decade. New credit provided through the Programa Nacional de Solidaridad (Pronasol, later known as Solidaridad) covered only half the production costs in this sector.

The transition to the free market in rural Mexico was governed by macroeconomic decisionmaking far removed from the realities of the campesinos. By the end of 1989 it was clear that the future of the agricultural sector would be subordinated to the economic goals of the Salinas administration: the reduction of inflation via wage and price controls, privatization of state enterprises and trade liberalization.

After 1989 only maize and beans continued to receive a guaranteed price. For other grains, such as sorghum, soy beans, rice, barley, wheat and safflower, guaranteed prices were replaced with a new scheme whereby prices were fixed through negotiations between the government, producers and buyers. However, the new scheme was implemented at the same time that import licenses were removed. This had catastrophic effects for many ejidatarios. In 1990, for example, thousands of soy bean and sorghum producers were unable to sell their crop due to the sudden inflow of cheaper

---

8. In this paper, "tons" refers to metric tons.

9. One piece of anecdotal evidence is the remark made by a campesino leader following a meeting with Banrural officials in Durango in the Fall of 1991. "It's funny", he said, "before we didn't know each other but there was always some money. Now we can talk face to face, but there is nothing!". The campesinos were requesting a loan to finance marketing of maize and beans. Banrural was in the process of pulling out of Durango.

grains from the United States. Campesinos in Sonora, Guanajuato and Tamaulipas protested by seizing government warehouses and blocking highways. In the case of sorghum, the final price which producers received was 20 percent lower than what had been agreed through the new scheme. Many switched back to maize production as all grain prices were depressed by the availability of cheap imports. This phenomenon extended to the entire agricultural sector.

The relative protection of maize and beans production was finally subordinated to the imperatives of free trade. Despite opposition from all national campesino organizations, the two crops were included in the negotiations leading to the NAFTA. Recognizing maize and beans as "sensitive crops" in the new free trade area, NAFTA provides for a fifteen-year phase-out of tariffs and import quotas. The rationale for NAFTA is that each country and region should produce goods and services in which they have comparative advantages. This argument implied that over two million small producers in Mexico could not continue to survive as maize producers. Average yields in Mexico are 1.7 tons per hectare, compared to 6.9 tons in the United States. Disparities in terms of technological development, subsidies, infrastructure and climatological factors also place Mexican producers at a great disadvantage (Calva 1992). These points were obviously not lost on the Zapatistas who timed their rebellion to coincide with the entry into effect of NAFTA.

In determining how many maize producers would lose from free trade, the crucial issue became the fixing of new pricing mechanisms. Under NAFTA the Mexican government decided that guaranteed prices would have to be phased out, allowing the international price to gradually take its place. After several months of debate, in October 1993 Salinas announced the Programa Nacional de Apoyos Directos al Campo (Procampo), described by the SARH as "a new support program for the Mexican farm sector" (SARH 1993).

Procampo and Pricing Policy for Maize

What were the main objectives of Procampo and what implications did they represent for maize producers in Chiapas? Under Procampo over 3.3 million producers of seven crops were made eligible for direct payments to be made on a per hectare basis.[10] All those who had planted one of these crops during the period between December 1990 and December 1993 and who had been included in a national directory compiled by SARH during 1993 could request payment of 330 new pesos (equivalent to US$103) for each hectare cultivated during the Autumn-Winter crop cycle of 1993-94. The payments were due to be made at the time of harvest in March 1994. One of the distinguishing features of Procampo is that it included 2.2 million farmers who produce solely for their own family's subsistence needs and had been isolated from official support, especially credit.

At first sight it would appear that campesinos in the Altos and Selva regions stand to gain from this new subsidy. These are maize deficit areas and the lowering of maize prices should theoretically lead to a reduction of hunger, especially in the Altos where yields can be as low as 0.5

These were maize, beans, sorghum, soy beans, rice, wheat, and cotton.

tons per hectare. The most negatively affected groups instead appear to be small and medium-sized ejidos in the Frailesca and Centro regions who depend on maize sales for a significant part of their income. This is not an insignificant sector. The proportion of total maize output in Chiapas which is sold on the market is twice as high as that consumed by the family unit. According to the SARH-CEPAL survey, 67 percent of maize production within the social sector of Chiapas is sold on the market, while 33 per cent goes to household consumption (SARH-CEPAL 1992, p.92). NAFTA and lower maize prices will therefore have a direct effect on thousands of producers that until 1994 depended on the guaranteed price.

In the case of poorer producers in the Altos and Selva, the potentially positive effects of falling prices may be cancelled out by political factors. In many remote districts local *caciques* exercise monopolistic control over transportation and marketing. Prices in Ocosingo or Altamirano may not come to reflect international prices at all if local merchants regulate the amount of maize available for purchase and at what price. In the absence of governmental regulation one possible alternative is to help grassroots orgnaizations develop their own food purchasing and distribution co-operatives, but this would require the type of political decision that has traditionally been lacking in Chiapas.

For its part, the Procampo subsidy is generally seen as a palliative in the Altos and Selva. The payments are simply used for any of several urgent necessities, such as the obtaining food, clothing or medical attention rather than providing a stimulus for production. In this way the subsidy tends to find its way back into the hands of the local merchants and private intermediaries which in turn control prices and distribution of basic goods. In sum, the changes in maize pricing policy may turn out to benefit merchants more than rural producers or consumers.

In the area of conflict mthe phasing out of guaranteed prices was seen as another indication of declining government support for ejido agriculture rather than representing a positive step to reduce food prices for consumers. Further research is necesssary to determine the precise impact of these changes as the tariffs on maize imports are phased out. The results may also determine the level of political support for the government and its rural reforms if the problem of hunger is seen to be improving or deteriorating under the new rules.

Procampo foresaw two stages of implementation. The transition phase would include two crop cycles: Autumn-Winter 1993-94 and Spring-Summer 1994. The Autumn-Winter 1994-95 cycle would mark the beginning of the definitive phase. Direct payments per hectare were to increase in the transition phase, and then remain constant in real terms for ten years, before being phased out completely by the year 2008. At the same time the guaranteed price would be replaced by the international price. How this transition takes place will determine the fate of millions of campesinos. The Chiapas rebellion will undoubtedly affect this process and opens up the possibility of designing alternative policies not just for the maize sector but for rural development as a whole.

Under Procampo, as several observers argued, short-term gains will be felt by small producers but the medium and long term trend will be exclusion from the market (Bartra 1993; Moguel 1993). This can be demonstrated by the incomes which are projected over the next three cycles. Table 3 shows how the expected transition to the international price (which includes transportation and storage costs of imported grain) negatively affects incomes of more productive farmers immediately and all maize farmers after April 1995. In line with the initial calculations of Procampo, it assumes that the international price per ton will fully replace the guaranteed price by the Autumn-Winter 1994-95 cycle.

The losses increase in direct proportion to productivity, which has the positive effect of reducing subsidies for large-scale farmers who are in a better position to produce more profitable items. However, Procampo also implies a disincentive to a large sector of ejidatarios who until 1994 supplied most of the national market. The implications for these producers are clear. They must either switch to more lucrative crops or increase the share of non-agricultural income coming into the household. Although Procampo allows its beneficiaries to continue to receive direct payments if they switch out of maize production, the cost of converting to export crops such as winter fruits and vegetables far exceeds the Procampo subsidies.[11]

The failure of Salinas's rural reforms to attract significant amounts of private investment into Mexican agriculture also suggests limitations to crop diversification, while the limited access to credit, insurance and technical assistance has already been noted. In 1993 less than 1 percent of foreign investment in Mexico went into agriculture. In addition, the decline in both public and private investment since 1982 is reflected in the deterioration of infrastructure, tractors and machinery. Without a serious program to promote integral rural development, which would inevitably imply a much greater role for campesino and indigenous organizations in planning and policy-making, initiatives such as Procampo will be ineffective in reversing rural decline.

The implications for producers in Chiapas are no less ominous. In 1990 over 166,000 ejidatarios, equivalent to 91 percent of the state's total, produced maize. Over 95 percent of the maize area is rain-fed, producing a similar proportion of total maize output. In the rainfed sector the average individual plot was 3.7 hectares, with average yields of 1.52 tons/hectare, equivalent to a total output of 5.6 tons. Prior to Procampo the guaranteed price for maize was 750 new pesos. Producers averaging an output of 5.6 tons in 1993 would have therefore received a total income of 4200 new pesos for that crop if they had access to the guaranteed price. If we take Table 3 as a guideline, the short and medium term impacts of Procampo in Chiapas become clear (Table 4).

---

11. This point was made with great clarity for the case of Sonora by David Runsten at the November 1993 workshop of the Ejido Reform Research Project in Tepotzlán. Ejidatarios had been given government figures which grossly underestimated the cost of converting to strawberry production which turned out to be two hundred times higher than what the Procampo subsidy provided.

Table 3

POTENTIAL WINNERS AND LOSERS AMONG MAIZE
PRODUCERS UNDER *Procampo*

A. Planned Maize Prices and Amounts of Direct Payments to Producers

Cropping Season[a] Year	A-W 1993-94	S-S 1994	A-W 1994-95
Price/ton[b]	650	600	450
Payment/hectare[b]	330	350	350

B. Expected Gross Revenue and (Net Change), by Yield Levels

Cropping Season Year	A-W 1993-94		S-S 1994		A-W 1994-95	
1 ton/hectare	980	(230)	950	(200)	800	(50)
2 ton/hectare	815	(130)	775	(50)	625	(- 250)
3 ton/hectare	760	(30)	716	(-102)	566	(- 552)
4 ton/hectare	732	(- 62)	687	(-252)	537	(- 852)
5 ton/hectare	716	(-170)	670	(-400)	520	(-1150)

> Source: Moguel 1993, p.9.
> Notes: a) A-W = Autumn-Winter, S-S = Spring-Summer
>   b) Prices and payments are in New Pesos, as of January 1994,
>   US$1.00 = N$3.15

Table 4

POTENTIAL IMPACT OF *Procampo* ON AVERAGE
MAIZE REVENUES IN CHIAPAS

Cropping Season Year	A-W 1993-94	S-S 1994	A-W 1994-95
Price component/5.6 mt	3640	3360	2520
Payment component/3.7 ha	1221	1295	1295
Total income	4861	4655	3926
Variations from 1993	661	465	-274

> Source: Based on planned maize prices and amounts of direct
> payments to producers as reported in Table 3.

Solidaridad and Political Control

The rural reforms were accompanied by the further expansion of Solidaridad, which was established by Salinas in December 1988 (and called originally Pronasol) and became incorporated within the Secretaría de Desarrollo Social (Sedesol) in 1992. Although Chiapas received more funds from Solidaridad than any other state, several observers noted that the resources were insufficient to ameliorate extensive and increasing poverty. A central limitation was that support for the production and marketing needs of the social sector was not given sufficient emphasis within the program.

According to official figures over 50 percent of the population suffers from malnutrition, one of the highest rates in the country. The state's illiteracy rate (30 percent) is three times higher than the national average, while the proportion of children who do not complete primary school is 62 percent, compared to 21 percent nationally. Overcrowded housing conditions affect around 80 percent of homes in the municipalities of Ocosingo, Altamirano and Las Margaritas. Other services are equally lacking (Table 5).

Solidaridad expenditure in Chiapas grew by 130 percent in 1989-90, 50 percent in 1990-91, 20 percent in 1991-92 and a further 1 percent in 1992-93 (Table 6). Most of the funding was designed to improve social welfare and public works, with only 12 percent going to support productive activities. This is especially important if we consider the impact of the rural reforms referred to above. In fact, according to the Coordinadora Nacional de Organizaciones Cafetaleras (CNOC) the amount of credit which coffee growers received from Solidaridad in 1993 was 13 percent less than in 1988 when INMECAFE was still operating (Cano 1994, p.6).[12] Landlessness and unemployment, especially among the young, have not been cushioned by Solidaridad. Under the program, each project has a low investment ceiling, allowing the government to reach a larger population with small projects but reducing their overall social impact. Proponents of a new anti-poverty program argue that larger projects, co-managed with representative local and regional social organizations, should instead be designed to attack the structural roots of poverty rather than its symptoms. Such a strategy would also bolster campesino organizations as counterweights to local elites. The Chiapas rebellion lends weight to this position by demonstrating both the limitations of Solidaridad itself and the need for a political opening to the benefit of campesino organizations in the state.

Although Chiapas ranks first in the number of local solidarity committees (8,824 or 8.26 percent of the national total), according to Moguel (1994) the figure is misleading since it includes any type of group which has received funds from the program. Most of these (7,474) participate in basic infrastructure and social welfare projects (Dignified Schools, Municipal Funds and Children

---

12. The CNOC emerged as an independent response to the collapse in the international price in 1989, although it has antecedents in the early 1980s (Moguel 1992a). By the end of 1993 it represented almost 60,000 small producers from seven states, including approximately 20,000 growers from Chiapas. Most of its member organizations were independent of the PRI and other political parties. According to its own census compiled in December 1993, in Chiapas there were forty local organizations participating in CNOC.

in Solidaridad). These tend to either have a short time-span between the disbursement of funds until the end of the project, or - as in the case of Municipal Funds - are very tightly controlled by the local political bosses, or *caciques*. One of the factors which contributed to divisions and unrest within indigenous communities was precisely the manipulation of Solidaridad funds by municipal presidents loyal to the PRI and the state governor.

Table 5
INDICES OF POVERTY IN CHIAPAS

Percentage of homes without

	electricity	drinking water	drainage
Mexico	12.5	20.6	36.4
Chiapas	33.1	41.6	58.8
Ocosingo	67.9	49.2	60.2
Altamirano	75.0	48.8	43.7
Las Margaritas	66.4	72.7	38.5

Sources: Data for Mexico and Chiapas are from INEGI 1992. Data for Ocosingo, Altamirano and Las Margaritas are drawn from the Consejo Nacional de Población (CONAPO) as cited in *La Jornada*, 3 January 1994, p.11.

Table 6

Pronasol EXPENDITURE IN CHIAPAS
(Thousands of New Pesos)

Year	Total	Solidaridad for production	Solidaridad for welfare	Infrastructure	Other
1989	95,743	12,338	46,530	29,659	7,216
1990	236,166	35,282	94,526	101,527	4,831
1991	371,366	48,258	130,188	183,666	9,254
1992	441,827	46,343	219,741	175,554	186
1993	445,709	48,562	277,537	119,333	277
Total	1,590,811	190,783	768,522	609,739	21,764

Source: Carlos Salinas de Gortari, *Quinto informe de gobierno (anexo)*, 1993. Cited in Moguel (1994, p.8).

This manipulation was promoted by governor Patrocinio González Garrido. For example, one of the programs designed to support subsistence farmers was the Credit on Demand scheme (Crédito a la Palabra).[13] This involved the disbursement of interest-free loans on an individual basis (principally to maize and beans producers) which, when paid back, were meant to be recycled in the form of new loans and investment in community welfare projects. Chiapas had the distinction of being the state with the highest loan repayment rate. In 1992, 88 percent of loans were repaid and over 70 percent had been recovered in 1993. However, the supposed benefits were not distributed equitably. Although loan repayment was highest in the Altos and Selva regions, the share of the state's "crédito a la solidaridad" which these regions received fell between 1990 and 1993 from 23 to 16 percent and from 17 to 6 percent, respectively.

Part of the explanation for this paradox was the governor's political control of the program. In other parts of Mexico the repayment of Solidaridad loans was used to generate new sources of financing for community projects. In Chiapas, by contrast, the governor created a state-level fund directly under his control. The disbursement of credit in this way favored political allies in the PRI and CNC, strengthening the control exercised by municipal presidents and marginalizing independent organizations. A state-level Ministry of Community Participation, staffed by loyal PRI and CNC leaders, was set up in early 1992 in an effort to institutionalize these arrangements.

The governor also dismissed officials who attempted to support local independent organizations. For example, in 1990 the regional director of the Instituto Nacional Indigenista (INI) in Las Margaritas was forced to resign after assisting the Unión de Ejidos de la Selva in its efforts to gain Solidaridad funding to purchase a coffee processing plant from INMECAFE. Then in March 1992 three top INI officials in Chiapas were arrested: the state director and the regional director and treasurer for the Tzeltal area. They were accused of corruption in the use of funds to support small-scale livestock activities in Ocosingo and Chilón. Local campesino leaders came out in their defense, arguing that their only crime was to have supported the projects of independent groups. Although they were later released none could return to their previous posts (*La Jornada*, 21 March 1992, p.13).

Solidaridad as a whole was not such a threat to González Garrido as he had feared. Yet his political aims compounded the program's own limitations and contributed to the anger which would be directed by the EZLN against municipal presidents. One of the immediate repercussions of the uprising was the resignation of the state delegate of Sedesol in January 1994. The new interim governor, Javier López Moreno also announced his intention to meet with municipal authorities to investigate the misuse of Solidaridad funds. During the first week of February 1994 several town halls were occupied by campesino groups calling for the dismissal of municipal presidents.[14]

---

13. Information contained in this section is drawn from Cano (1994). In Chiapas the program was renamed "Crédito a la Solidaridad" by González Garrido.

14. The announcement in August 1993 of a further US$55 million for social projects in the border region of Chiapas obviously came too late to forestall the rebellion. Solidaridad moneys were also allegedly used for such non-priority works as the construction of hundreds of basketball courts, a sumptuous Convention Center in Tuxtla Gutiérrez, and the refurbishment of central parks and town halls (Hughes 1994).

III. EJIDO REFORM AND THE AGRARIAN QUESTION IN CHIAPAS

The most disputed of Salinas's rural reforms was the decision to modify Article 27 of the Mexican Constitution. This article enshrined the central gains of the Zapatistas in the 1910-17 Revolution and laid the basis for agrarian reform over the next seventy years. By 1991 there were a total of 29,951 ejidos and comunidades agrarias in Mexico, representing half of the country's land surface and 3.5 million families or 20 million people, equivalent to a quarter of the country's population (PROCEDE 1993, p.10). Before considering the precise nature of the reforms and how they were perceived in Chiapas it is important to understand the centrality of agrarian struggles in the shaping campesino consciousness in the state.

Land Reform, Campesino Struggles and Repression, 1982-1993

Land reform in Mexico followed different patterns according to local and regional factors. In Chiapas political resistance to redistribution originated in the pacts made between local elites and the post-revolutionary governments of the center. During 1914-1920 lowland ranchers and estate owners organized a successful counter-revolution and one of their leaders, Tiburcio Fernández Ruiz, became governor in 1920 (Benjamin 1989, pp.95-143). He decreed that individual private owners would be allowed to keep up to 8,000 hectares of land.[15] Major changes were not seen until the Cárdenas presidency (1934-40) but even then the new beneficiaries received generally marginal land of low productivity or became a captive labor market for large coffee plantations (García de León 1985). Outside of this exceptional conjuncture, agrarian reform in Chiapas was never based on the actual redistribution of private holdings but on colonization of unused forested areas in the Selva region (Reyes Ramos 1992, p.62).

During the 1970s and 1980s an increase in land invasions was met with violent repression but the government was also forced to purchase land from large owners for the purpose of redistribution (Fernández Ortiz and Tarrío García 1983, pp.140-151; Benjamin 1989, pp.223-243; Harvey 1990). As in other states with high indigenous populations, in Chiapas land reform was forced back onto the political agenda in the early 1980s by the persistence of new campesino organizations. It would be false to say that land reform was avoided in the 1980s. A redistribution program was in fact effective in providing over 80,000 hectares of land for over 9,000 campesinos. However, the way in which it was implemented created more conflicts than it solved.

In 1984 the state government of Absalón Castellanos Domínguez signed agreements with the federal Agrarian Reform Minister to implement a plan to resolve land disputes in Chiapas. The plan, known as the Programa de Rehabilitación Agraria (PRA), was designed to purchase land which

---

15. Article 1 of the Ley Agraria del Estado de Chiapas of 1921 stipulated that "The term latifundio refers to all properties which exceed 8,000 hectares, held by an individual person *or by a company (sociedad) that has the legal capacity to acquire ownership*" (emphasis added). It is ironic that in 1994 a group of twenty-five individuals associated in a *sociedad mercantil* can own up to 10,000 hectares of good quality pasture land without being considered latifundistas, at least by the law.

belonged to private owners but which had been occupied by campesinos whose claims for distribution had not been resolved by the Secretaria de Reforma Agraria (SRA). These lands would then be officially given ejido status.

The areas chosen for "rehabilitation" were obviously those with the greatest number of land invasions. Since these tended to be led by the independent organizations, the official CNC feared they would be strengthened and began to dispute ownership of the same lands, even carrying out its own land invasions in PRA targeted zones. One of the most important areas for the PRA was Simojovel on the northern edge of the Altos region. Since the mid-1970s former workers on coffee plantations had been organized by supporters of the Central Independiente de Obreros Agrícolas y Campesinos (CIOAC). By 1981 the CIOAC had built an important base of support and organized strikes on over forty plantations in demand of improved working conditions, wages and respect for labor rights. When no solutions were given, the CIOAC began to press instead for the redistribution of the fincas into ejidos (Pontigo Sánchez 1985). With the announcement of the PRA, land which was in possession of CIOAC supporters and awaiting regularization was then invaded by CNC supporters. Violent conflicts between the two groups became inevitable and continued well into the following administration.

The PRA targeted 41 municipalities (over a third of the state's total) grouped in six zones (the northern part of Los Altos, Fronteriza, Centro, Costa, Frailesca and the Selva). The four municipalities that saw most redistribution were, as the Program intended, those with a recent history of land conflicts: Simojovel and Bochil in the northern Altos, Ocosingo in the Selva and Venustiano Carranza in the Centro region. However, the independent organizations in each area did not receive the share of land which corresponded to their demands or their size. In Simojovel and Bochil the CIOAC received title to 16 ejidos, compared to 30 for the CNC. In Ocosingo 17 ejidos were distributed among campesinos without affiliation but promoted by the CNC, compared to only one for the largest independent group in the area, the Unión de Uniones Ejidales y Grupos Campesinos Solidarios de Chiapas (UU). In Venustiano Carranza the Organización Campesina Emiliano Zapata (OCEZ) did not receive any land at all under the PRA. Rather than solve disputes the PRA had the effect of transforming conflicts between campesinos and landowners into conflicts between independent organizations and the CNC (Reyes Ramos 1992, pp.113-118).

The principal beneficiaries of the PRA were the landowners and some agrarian reform officials. On the one hand, the former received payment for land which they had resigned themselves to losing anyway. In the process the conflict for them had been defused as different groups of campesinos now battled with each other over land ownership. On the other, the program provided opportunities for corruption and personal enrichment. Landowners invented "land invasions" on their property, appealing to the state government to purchase the disputed land. Some officials colluded by paying out "compensation" for lands which were never to be distributed and, as part of the corruption, retained some of the money for themselves. The program was suspended in the summer of 1985, less than a year after it had begun, when the federal government ordered an investigation. In order to show that the PRA was still necessary the state government began to evict members of the UU from allegedly disputed lands in Ocosingo. In August 1985 four communities were evicted by state police, leading to protests and a march by over 2,000 Tzeltal Indians to Tuxtla Gutiérrez. The UU was able to uphold its argument that the communities in question already had legal documents. However, the PRA did return in 1985 and continued until its US$100 million budget expired in 1987.

Land petitioners also came up against increasing repression. State police and local CNC groups were involved in numerous attacks on members of independent organizations. In October 1984 nine OCEZ members were killed in an ambush by CNC supporters in Venustiano Carranza. In the following year two demonstrations by CIOAC and OCEZ were violently broken up by state police. The CIOAC also blamed CNC members at the command of Ernesto Castellanos, brother of the state governor, for the murder of one of their lawyers, Andulio Gálvez in August 1985. Nor were CNC leaders who opposed the government treated any differently. In May 1986, Germán Jiménez, a former PRI deputy and CNC leader, was arrested and imprisoned for his part in protests by thousands of maize producers demanding higher crop prices. Finally, in December 1987 seven people were killed when Security Police broke up demonstrations by OCEZ and CIOAC campesinos at the municipal palaces of Simojovel and La Independencia. At the same time police ransacked a house in Comitán used by Maryknoll nuns who had allegedly supported the protests. Evictions of alleged land invaders increased as the administration drew to a close.

The Castellanos Domínguez government also helped protect private landowners from possible expropriation by issuing more *certificados de inafectabilidad* (documents of inaffectability) than all the previous state governors combined. The main beneficiaries were the private ranchers who were issued with 4,714 *certificados*, equivalent to 95 percent of the total number distributed in the state since 1934. By the end of this administration at least 70 percent of the area used by cattle ranchers was legally beyond the reach of agrarian reform (Reyes Ramos 1992, p.119).

When a new governor took office in December 1988 many hoped that a more conciliatory approach would replace the repression. In his electoral campaign Patrocinio González Garrido echoed the *salinista* discourse of consensus-building. However, the first three months of his administration saw the assassination of several members of independent organizations, including two of the principal campesino leaders in the state: Sebastián Pérez Núñez of the CIOAC and Arturo Albores Velasco of the OCEZ. González Garrido denied government involvement but human rights activists criticized the impunity of these and other actions. Nevertheless, the governor was forced to address the agrarian question.

In 1989 seven cases were targeted for negotiated solutions. These involved the return of communal lands in Venustiano Carranza, Nicolás Ruiz and Villa Corzo and the titling of ejido land in El Carrizal (Ocosingo), San Sebastián Bachajón (Chilón), Unión Calera (Arriaga) and San Juan Chamula. Although these cases were partially resolved, there were another 547 cases still awaiting resolution in 1989, representing 22,598 land claimants (SRA 1989). Furthermore, although the governor had to deal with independent organizations in resolving these cases, once the agreements had been made no further opening was offered. On the contrary, as land conflicts continued to occur throughout the state, the governor reverted to the traditionally repressive tactics of his predecessors.

For example, several settlements in the municipality of Chiapa de Corzo were destroyed by state police and landowners on two separate occasions in April 1990 and April 1991. Members of the OCEZ claimed that the disputed lands were in fact covered by a presidential resolution in their favor. In June 1990 six people were injured when private gunmen shot at a crowd of over one hundred cane producers who were demanding full payment for cane delivered to the Pujiltic sugar mill. In July of the same year women from the highland settlement of San Felipe Ecatepec staged a hunger strike in Mexico City's Zócalo to demand a hearing with the President. They protested the repression of their organization, the Coordinadora Nacional de Pueblos Indígenas (CNPI) at the hands of the state government. In October 1990 two members of OCEZ were injured when unknown assailants opened fire on a peaceful march from Venustiano Carranza to Tuxtla Gutiérrez (Horizontes 1990, 1991a, 1991b).

In July 1991 a protest march by 300 Indians from the Selva Lacandona was broken up by police in Palenque using clubs and tear gas grenades. Seven leaders were arrested and forced to sign confessions linking them to Central American guerrillas and drug-trafficking. They were protesting the illegal confiscation of timber by state police and the corruption of municipal authorities (Harvey 1992a). Finally, in September 1991 the parish priest of Simojovel, Joel Padrón, was arrested on charges of robbery, damages to property and provocations. The roots of what became a political conflict between the state government and the local Catholic Church were to be found in the type of conflicts generated by the PRA. Campesinos belonging to a CNC group claimed that members of the CIOAC had evicted them from their land with the help of Joel Padrón. The state government attempted to condition the release of Padrón to a series of commitments from the Bishop of San Cristóbal, Mgr. Samuel Ruiz García, to order the eviction of alleged land invasions and declare his opposition to actions against private property. Ruiz was also requested to drop charges against police for the illegal detention of Joel Padrón and that he order Padrón to leave Chiapas once released (Aguilar Zinser 1991). Although these conditions were not accepted and charges against Padrón were eventually dropped, they were a clear indication of the governor's openness to the demands of ranchers and landowners. They also reaffirmed the central role of Samuel Ruiz, the Diocese of San Cristóbal and the Centro de Derechos Humanos "Fray Bartolomé de las Casas" in defending indigenous rights.

Political pressure against the Church increased in 1993. In March of that year two soldiers were killed in the Tzotzil community of San Isidro El Ocotal in Los Altos. Members of the community feared that the clandestine use of local timber would be discovered by the army and the two soldiers were mistakenly identified as forestry agents.[16] The Centro de Derechos Humanos "Fray Bartolomé de las Casas" denounced the killings but also denounced the abuse of human rights carried out by soldiers in the arrest of thirteen suspects who were allegedly subjected to torture. Police returned to the community on two further occasions in April and May 1993 and carried out further illegal arrests and beatings. The original thirteen were eventually released without charges

---

16. Despite a 1989 ban on exploitation of forestry resources in Chiapas, this activity has continued due to the lack of adequate alternative sources of income. Moreover, the ban has led to several conflicts with the police and army. The July 1991 protests in the Selva, referred to above, originated in application of the 1989 decree.

being brought against them (Minnesota Advocates for Human Rights 1993, pp. 10-16). During the rest of 1993 political pressure against the Diocese of San Cristóbal increased, culminating in the efforts of the Papal representative to remove Samuel Ruiz from his position in Chiapas. The outbreak of the rebellion frustrated this move as Ruiz became a key mediator in negotiations between the EZLN and the government.

The Ejido Reform and Potential Effects in Chiapas

The reforms to Article 27 of the Constitution were proposed in November 1991 and adopted just two months later. They were followed in late February 1992 by the passage of a new Agrarian Law to establish the new regulatory framework for the social sector. For the government the modifications were seen as necessary steps to attract private investment in agriculture and increase productivity and welfare. Four of the main changes embodied in the new Agrarian Law were the following:

1. Ejidatarios were given the legal right to purchase, sell, rent or use as collateral the individual plots and communal lands which make up the ejido.
2. Private companies were allowed to purchase land in accordance with the legal limits ascribed to different crops. At a maximum, a company with at least twenty-five individual share-holders could purchase holdings of up to twenty-five times the size of the individually permitted limit.
3. The reforms also allowed for new associations between capitalists and ejidatarios, the latter providing land as "T" shares in joint ventures.
4. In line with the reform's intention of guaranteeing security for private property, the sections of Article 27 which allowed for campesinos to petition for land redistribution were deleted from the new law.

The debate surrounding the ejido reform raised several concerns. Firstly, it was feared that the sale of ejido plots could lead to a reconcentration of land. Although the new law expressly forbids *latifundios* in Mexico, it also potentially allows for private companies of at least twenty-five individuals to own farms of up to 2,500 hectares of irrigated land, 5,000 hectares in the case of rainfed areas, 10,000 hectares of good quality pasture land or 20,000 hectares of forested land. A company made up of 25 ranchers could also feasibly own an area equivalent to 12,500 hectares. In order for ejido land to be made available for private ownership, however, the assembly of ejido members must approve the measure by a two-thirds majority. Some commentators noted that the traditional control and manipulation of assemblies by ejido authorities could lead to forced votes in favor of privatization (Moguel 1992b, p.273). In Chiapas the potential for land reconcentration is given by the politically powerful ranchers' associations, representing over 12,000 *ganaderos* organized in sixty local associations. Ranchers applauded the reforms to Article 27, arguing that greater security in land tenure would attract foreign investors wishing to create new meat processing plants in the region. The competition for land with indigenous campesinos should be understood in this context (*El Financiero,* 10 June 1993, p.46).

Secondly, the use of land as collateral or in associations with private investors involved the risk of farm foreclosures and loss of land rights. The effective exclusion of much of the social sector from traditional sources of credit could influence the decisions of ejidatarios in putting land up as collateral. Women were placed at most risk since the male head of household could unilaterally decide how to dispose of what was family patrimony. The only special right which women received was the first option to buy the ejido land which their spouses decided to sell. In Chiapas it is possible that wealthier *ejidatarios* might concentrate land within communities as a result of foreclosures.

Finally, it was feared that most of the unresolved land petitions (*rezago agrario*) would simply be rejected. The government's claim that there was no more land to be distributed was contested by several organizations. Some called for an investigation into private holdings which allegedly exceeded the legal limits, prior to decreeing the end to land redistribution. It is significant that this demand was taken up by the campesino movement in Chiapas and reasserted in light of the Zapatista rebellion (*La Jornada*, 1 February 1994, p.5). In fact, rather than providing for the immediate expropriation and redistribution of excess holdings, the new law gave private owners one year to sell off excess property (Moguel 1992b, p.271). The end of land reform in Chiapas and other states also canceled out the hope of a piece of land for thousands of campesinos. In this respect, we should distinguish between effects which are directly measurable in terms of land purchases, etc. and those which operate more at the level of expectations, hopes and fears. It seems clear that the end of land reform constituted a symbolic break with the past but one which offered no guarantees of improvement for the future.

The Ejido Reform in Chiapas

As in most areas of rural Mexico, the immediate response to Salinas's announcement of ejido reform was one of fear and confusion. Information about the precise nature of the reforms was scarce and the immediate problems facing ejidatarios were increasing debts, falling prices for their crops and the lack of credit. However, two demonstrations against the reforms were held in December 1991 and January 1992. The first was led by the OCEZ in Venustiano Carranza, the second by the Asociación Rural de Interés Colectivo Unión de Uniones (ARIC) in Ocosingo. The members of the ARIC also made a formal commitment not to sell ejido land.

The Diocese of San Cristóbal also invited different organizations to reflect on the reforms at a special workshop held in January 1992. The workshop concluded that the ejido reform was part of the government's general strategy in favor of private capital; the spirit of the original law had been broken as the public interest was subordinated to individual interests; that the reconcentration of land in few hands was likely; and that it reflected the objectives of the proposed NAFTA. In political, economic and cultural terms the workshop saw only a deterioration of existing conditions. A more specific fear referred to the deepening of divisions within communities as village *caciques* moved to buy up land from poorer neighbors (Taller de San Cristóbal 1992).

The direct effects of ejido reform were only gradually emerging by the end of 1993. According to officials of the Registro Agrario Nacional (RAN) only 100 of the state's 2,072 ejidos had requested the assistance of the government's certification program PROCEDE (Interview, Registro Agrario Nacional, Mexico City, January 1994). The main problem with the reform concerned the lack of solution to a backlog of land petitions, known as the *rezago agrario*. Although in 1992 the state government announced that it would purchase land in order to deal with the *rezago*, the program did not advance. Campesino leaders blamed the delays on bureaucratic inefficiency, the reluctance of private owners to sell and collusion between functionaries and landowners.

In the Selva region the lack of definitive titles is a major problem for many communities. Not only does the lack of legal definition increase the possibility of eviction by landowners or other campesino groups, it also restricts access to credit. This obstacle hindered those ejidos which began to devote more land area to livestock in the 1980s (Leyva Solano and Ascencio Franco, 1993, p.274). The lack of secure titles further weakened the social organizations located in the area of rebellion.

The ARIC Unión de Uniones was particularly affected. During 1992 its leaders proposed several measures to deal with the agrarian problem. In addition to its existing legal petitions, the ARIC offered to buy land and asked for the redistribution of private estates which had been declared bankrupt. None of these proposals were taken up by the state government. For the president of the ARIC, the reason was a familiar one: "the agrarian authorities are friends of the landowners. They carry out their studies and reject our petitions. In this past year we have got nowhere. The landowners are refusing to sell and the Agraria says the ranchers all have documents protecting themselves from expropriation. This is the case in Patihuitz, Avellanal and La Estrella" (Interview, January 1993). It is no coincidence that the EZLN has been able to recruit campesinos in precisely these sub-regions of the Selva.

IV. GRASSROOTS ORGANIZING AND CAMPESINO RADICALISM

The EZLN was able to gain support from thousands of Tzeltal, Tzotzil,Zoque, Chol and Tojolobal Indians in Altos and Selva regions. It was not a movement implanted from outside but the most recent expression of popular organizing and resistance to elite manipulation, government indifference and police brutality. It drew support from campesinos who had participated over several years in legal organizations which sought to defend land rights and obtain more favorable terms for marketing their coffee. It was the denial of political space to these organizations which allowed for the armed option to gain acceptance.

Colonization and Social Organization in the Selva

The largest base of support for the EZLN came from indigenous communities located in the Selva region. Many of these had been established over a period of forty years of colonization. The flow of migrants to the Selva began in the 1930s but increased rapidly after 1950. Colonization was encouraged as a means to avoid affecting the interests of private owners in other parts of Chiapas. By 1970 an estimated 100,000 migrants had settled in the region, principally Tzeltal, Chol and Tojolobal Indians. These were former plantation workers from the northern and eastern highlands or campesinos who had lost land due to the encroachments of local elites (Ramos Hernández 1978, p.26). The population of Ocosingo, the region's largest municipality, more than doubled between 1950 and 1970, doubled again in 1970-80 and grew by another 56 percent in 1980-90 (Ascencio Franco and Leyva Solano 1992, p.204).

As a result of colonization the area controlled by large estates declined, while the ejido sector increased its presence. Between 1930 and 1991 over 1.3 million hectares were distributed among 25,000 campesinos in Ocosingo, Altamirano and Las Margaritas (Ascencio Franco and Leyva Solano 1992, p.217). Ranchers continued to dominate the region's economy however since they controlled the best pasture lands, most of the cattle and capital. With the crisis in coffee production many of the ejidos also turned to raising livestock in association with private ranchers. In 1990 a survey of 3,500 campesino families in the region found that 60 percent of land had been converted to pasture, 30 percent was used for maize and beans and only 10 percent was dedicated to coffee (Ascencio Franco and Leyva Solano 1992, pp.192-4). Many campesinos came to depend on ranchers for temporary work on estates, clear new areas of pasture land or enter into co-operative associations (Leyva Solano and Ascencio Franco 1993, p.273). However, as with coffee, livestock also proved to be vulnerable to the economic reforms and trade liberalization and cheaper imports. In addition, between 1980 and 1990 demographic growth in this region exceeded that for the state as a whole. Whereas the average annual rate for Chiapas in this period was 4.4 percent, the rate for Ocosingo was 5.6 percent and for Las Margaritas 7.4 percent. Altamirano registered a slightly lower rate of 3.4 percent (Ascencio Franco and Leyva Solano 1992, p.204).

The first institutions to organize the colonists in the Selva Lacandona were religious bodies. From the 1940s Protestant missionaries associated with the Summer Institute of Linguistics were invited by the government to assist in the acculturation of the region's indigenous population (Dichtl 1987, p.45). Traditional cultural practices were discouraged, while individual effort and conversion to new crops were fomented. Government support for Protestant sects continued in subsequent decades as it attempted to limit the influence of Catholic priests and liberation theology. The region's population which considered itself Protestant increased from less than 5 percent in 1960 to 25 percent in 1990 (Ascencio Franco and Leyva Solano 1992, p.211).

Catholic missionaries began to work in the Selva in the late 1960s, but adopted a different approach to that of their Protestant counterparts. Its priests and catechists sought to rescue and restore the centrality of indigenous traditions and practices and promoted the formation of local co-operatives. This approach reflected the "preferential option for the poor" which the Diocese of San Cristóbal had begun to promote at the time of the Medellín Council of Latin American Bishops in

1968. Mgr. Samuel Ruiz, Bishop of the Diocese since 1960, participated in the Medellín conference and became an important proponent of an autochthonous, popular Church.

Prior to Medellín the Diocese had already begun to adapt its own structures, creating special teams of priests assigned to regions inhabited by the four largest indigenous groups (Tzeltal, Tzotzil, Chol and Tojolobal) and two predominantly mestizo areas in the center and border regions. This reorganization proved to be important when, in 1971, the state government requested that the Church organize an Indian Congress to commemorate the quincentenary of the death of Fray Bartolomé de las Casas. Preparation for the Congress involved the formation of community-level groups to elaborate their specific complaints, demands and proposals around the four main issues of land tenure, marketing, education and health. The Church invited students and professors to assist catechists in providing courses in agrarian law, economics, Mexican history and agronomy. Out of this process a new generation of indigenous community leaders emerged with a different perspective on the causes of poverty and injustice. Whereas conflicts had previously been understood in terms of personal relations, the participants in the Congress began to see the broader structural forces at work.

The Congress was held in San Cristóbal de las Casas in October 1974. 587 Tzeltal delegates, 330 Tzotziles, 152 Tojolobales and 161 Choles were present, representing 327 communities (Mestries 1990, p.473). On agrarian matters, delegates demanded the titling of ejido and communal land and denounced encroachment by ranchers. Plantation workers, newly aware of their labor rights, demanded respect for the provisions of the Federal Labor Code such as the minimum wage. Others called for greater access to markets, complaining how local intermediaries controlled credit, prices and transportation. Delegates also demanded education in their own languages and the defense of indigenous cultures. Finally, poor sanitation and the lack of medical services and clinics outside of the main towns were denounced as responsible for high indices of disease and infant mortality which was estimated at 42 deaths per thousand births in 1970 (Mestries 1990; Morales Bermúdez 1992).

Maoism in the Selva

The Congress proved to be a catalyst for grassroots organizing in the Altos and Selva. Its impact was felt most in the Selva region. This was probably due to the weaker presence of governmental institutions outside of the central highlands. In the central part of the Altos the INI, CNC and PRI had succeeded in undermining traditional forms of indigenous organization and in extending vertical and clientelistic lines of control (Wasserstrom 1983, p.178; Rus, forthcoming). In the more peripheral and dispersed settlements of the Selva, the Catholic priests and catechists were able to build support for more autonomous forms of representation. This is important in understanding the process of popular organization in the Selva. The origins are more social than institutional. Organization followed an intense period of political learning, achieved through a shared social and religious identification. Consequently, when the government began to promote the formation of Uniones de Ejidos in Chiapas, the new UEs which emerged in the Selva were not controlled by interests loyal to the PRI but by the delegates who had participated in the Indian

Congress.[17] In this respect, the three most important cases were the UE "Quiptic Ta Lecubtecel" (United by our Strength, in Tzeltal), (Ocosingo), UE Tierra y Libertad and UE Lucha Campesina (Las Margaritas), each of which were "formed" by the SRA in 1976.

The largest of these was the UE Quiptic which represented eighteen communities located in the Valley of San Quintín, Ocosingo. Among the advisers which the Church had invited to help prepare for the Indian Congress were activists from the Maoist group, Unión del Pueblo (UP). These advisers were important in bringing to the attention of Quiptic members the possible threat of eviction facing twenty-six communities in the region. This was due to a presidential resolution issued in March 1972 which gave sole land rights for over 660,000 hectares to just sixty-six lacandón families. However, the designated Comunidad Lacandona included at least 3,000 Tzeltal and Chol families who had settled in the area with government approval in the previous decades. Behind the decree was an agreement between the representatives of the lacandón Indians and the state-owned forestry company which allowed for the latter to exploit 35,000 cubic meters of mahogany and cedar for a period of ten years. The UP advisers began to warn of possible evictions in 1973 and this issue contributed to the decision to form the UE Quiptic.

Other advisers arrived in 1977 to organize the struggle against the land evictions. They also belonged to a Maoist political current known as Política Popular (PP) and arrived after hearing of an armed clash at Nueva Providencia, one of the threatened ejidos, in July 1977. The conflict had arisen when the local cacique kidnapped the son of an ejidatario who had begun to participate in the Quiptic. When the authorities failed to reply to appeals for his release a group of several hundred ejidatarios armed with machetes and rifles attacked the house where the boy was being kept. In the shoot-out seven police officers were killed, the cacique was taken prisoner and the boy freed. Groups of campesinos closed down nearby landing strips to avoid repression (Interview, adviser to UE Quiptic, October 1987).

Política Popular has its roots in the 1968 student movement and its principal leader was Adolfo Oribe Berlinguer, an economics professor at the Universidad Nacional Autónoma de México (the national university). In November 1968 Oribe wrote a pamphlet entitled "Hacia una política popular" ("Towards a Politics of the People"), which criticized the traditional left in Mexico for its lack of insertion among the masses. Seeking to apply the Maoist "mass line" to Mexico in a non-violent struggle for socialism, brigades of students went out to poor urban neighborhoods and ejidos to build bases of popular power at the grassroots. The most significant advances were made in the northern cities of Monterrey, Torreón and Chihuahua and among ejidatarios in La Laguna and Nayarit. In 1976 the PP joined with other groups, including Unión del Pueblo, to become known as Línea Proletaria (LP), which also developed an important presence in national unions of teachers, telephone workers and metalworkers. The arrival of LP activists in Chiapas was therefore part of a broad movement to build new forms of popular organization in Mexico. It should be stressed that

---

17. Uniones de Ejidos are second-level organizations which unite two or more ejidos as productive units. During the Echeverría presidency (1970-6), the government promoted the formation of UE's as a way to increase productivity in the social sector. Under new legislation preferential credit was to be channeled to those ejidos which joined together in second-level organizations. On the limitations of this strategy see Moguel and López Sierra (1990).

they did not promote armed struggle. In fact, one of their central strategic decisions, the "política de dos caras", was to avoid confrontations with the state, earning the criticism of many on the Left who concluded that LP was *gobiernista*.

The "norteños" from LP were not immediately accepted by the indigenous leaders who had the support of the Church. Sensing that the advisers were attempting to displace them as leaders they refused to co-operate and forced them to withdraw at the end of 1978. The advisers complained that the Church gave too much power to the same leaders who had been delegates at the 1974 Congress, creating a new clique rather than fostering grassroots participation. Some of the methods which the advisers tried to introduce undermined the centralization of decision-making. One was to revive a traditional element of indigenous democracy, the division of community assemblies into "small assemblies" or *asambleas chicas*. These were each made up of six or seven people who discussed problems or proposals which were then forwarded to the community assembly. A second strategy was to create horizontal links between the members of each community, rather than simply between the leaders or delegates. Drawing on their Maoist training they promoted contacts and exchanges between different communities at a grassroots level. Through a method known as "de las masas a las masas", commissions were sent to inform other communities of the threat of eviction from their land. This was painstaking work, involving treks of several days to reach distant settlements.

Despite the divisions between outside advisers and local leaders, the UE Quiptic continued to grow. In March 1978 a group of eight hundred campesinos blocked further construction of a perimeter road which was designed to delineate the Comunidad Lacandona. From that moment the organization expanded rapidly as ejidos to the north and east of Ocosingo also joined in the struggle to defend their land rights.

In 1979 the advisers were able to reincorporate themselves in the UE Quiptic. This was due to their promotion of a state-wide movement to improve the terms of coffee marketing for campesino producers. Two main problems were identified: the high cost of transporting coffee was absorbed by the producer and INMECAFE delayed paying producers for their crop. During 1979 several coffee growers' organizations, including the UE Quiptic, pressed INMECAFE to respond. A partial solution was achieved in November 1979 when an accord was signed in which INMECAFE agreed to pay 50 and 100 percent of air and ground transport costs, respectively.

The convergence around coffee marketing culminated in the formation in September 1980 of the Unión de Uniones Ejidales y Grupos Campesinos Solidarios de Chiapas (UU). The UU brought together the three Uniones de Ejidos which had been formed in 1976 and other smaller producer groups from the Altos, Selva and Fronteriza regions. This was the first and largest independent campesino organization in Chiapas, representing 12,000 mainly indigenous families from 180 communities in eleven municipalities (Harvey 1992b).[18]

---

18. These were Ocosingo, Las Margaritas, Tila, Sabanilla, Huitiupán, El Bosque, Larrainzar, Yajalón, Comitán, Frontera Comalapa and Motozintla.

The state government of Juan Sabines unsuccessfully attempted to co-opt the leaders of the new organization. However, internal differences between advisers split the UU into two camps in 1983. The Quiptic leaders accused Adolfo Oribe of attempting to rush through approval of the creation of a Credit Union for the UU and of by-passing internal democractic procedures. The Quiptic and two other Uniones de Ejidos pulled out of this alliance and, keeping the name Unión de Uniones, continued to work together until they formed a third-level organization in March 1988: the ARIC Unión de Uniones. The smaller groups from the Altos and Fronteriza regions operated the Unión de Crédito Pajal Ya'Kac'Tic in San Cristóbal de las Casas.

For the UE Quiptic, its participation in the UU had helped it to defend the land rights of the twenty-six communities still threatened with eviction. In October 1981 the UU led a march of 3,000 of its members to Tuxtla Gutiérrez to demand the suspension of eviction orders. The lack of guaranteed ejido titles continued to undermine the efforts of the UE Quiptic to promote economic projects. This contrasted with the Pajal Credit Union which expanded its operations rapidly from 1982 until the collapse in coffee prices in 1989.

Politically, the institutionalist strategy favored by the ARIC was increasingly seen as ineffective. Economically, the coffee sector was in crisis and ARIC had failed to develop a viable alternative in this region. The 1989 forestry ban removed another source of income. The turn to small-scale ranching demanded less labor and the fall in meat prices undercut even this activity. Finally, most of the energies of the ARIC were spent in agrarian litigation. Although the titles of the twenty-six ejidos in the Comunidad Lacandona were finally issued in January 1989, the delay had taken its toll on the members. Furthermore, there were many other land petitions awaiting solutions.

Despite deteriorating economic and social conditions, campesino organizations demonstrated their capacity to respond to crises on several occasions, suggesting the cohesive strength of inter-community relations gradually built up over a period of twenty years. For example, in response to the evictions of four ejidos on August 11, 1985 12,000 campesinos demonstrated in Ocosingo just two days later. Three days later 2,500 protesters had marched to Tuxtla Gutiérrez. The ability of the ARIC to carry out its own census and put forward plans for regional development is also evidence of the level of social organization in the area (Ascencio Franco and Leyva Solano 1992, pp.239-241).

There are many other sources of campesino radicalism in Chiapas. Between 1976 and 1989 the Tzotzil community of Venustiano Carranza fought a bitter struggle to recuperate over 3,000 hectares of prime land from local ranchers. Although the community had been issued in 1965 with a presidential resolution in its favor, ranchers deployed their own gunmen to evict campesinos from the disputed land. Twenty-five members of the community were killed between 1965 and 1985, while many others were imprisoned. In 1980 the community joined the Coordinadora Nacional Plan de Ayala (CNPA), a network of campesino and indigenous groups whose main demands were for land and an end to repression. In 1982 it joined with other local organizations to form the Organización Campesina Emiliano Zapata (OCEZ). At the end of the 1980s the OCEZ split into two factions. The group in Venustiano Carranza had left the CNPA and begun to work with a rival organization, the Frente Nacional Democrático Popular (FNDP). Both factions of the OCEZ displayed mistrust of all political parties and electoral struggles, distancing themselves from opposition left parties whom they regarded as reformist. The news of revolutionary movements in Central America was much more influential than in the case of the Unión de Uniones. The OCEZ leaders in Carranza also tended to prefer more visible public acts of protest than negotiations, bringing it into several violent confrontations with state police. As noted in the above discussion on agrarian struggles in the 1980s, the OCEZ and the CIOAC represented strong independent voices in the defense of campesino rights. During the early 1990s this type of radicalism was accompanied by the mobilization of new groups around the assertion of ethnicity.

Until 1992 events in Chiapas had largely escaped national attention. However that began to change with a march of four hundred Indians from Palenque to Mexico City in early 1992. The catalyst was another violent eviction by state police, this time of members of the Comité de Defensa de la Libertad Indígena (CDLI) who had gathered in Palenque on 28 December 1991. Their protest was to draw attention to the corruption of municipal presidents, the imposition of village authorities (*agentes municipales*), the failure of the government to carry out promised public works, the lack of solution to the *rezago agrario* and their opposition to the reforms to Article 27. Over one hundred were arrested and several people were beaten and tortured. The government used a 1989 reform to the state Penal Code in breaking up the demonstration. Articles 129 through 135 of this code classified participation in unarmed mass protests as threats to public order which were liable to punishments of two to four years imprisonment.

The "Xi'Nich" march left Palenque on March 7, 1992 and arrived in the capital six weeks later.[19] In the meantime they received national coverage in the independent press and solidarity from communities in Tabasco, Veracruz, Puebla and the state of Mexico. Its impact on national consciousness was to display the repressive nature of the state government in Chiapas. It also coincided with a growing awareness regarding the conditions of indigenous peoples in the country (Cepeda Neri 1992; Reyes Heroles 1992; Bellinghausen 1992). Yet, although Xi'Nich was able to gain promises of solutions from federal agencies, by the end of 1992 several of the demands had not been met. The state's Penal Code was not reformed; no police officers were ever brought to trial for alleged human rights abuses; and municipal presidents continued to impose *agentes municipales*. There were still thirty arrest orders out against CDLI members and new public works had not begun.

It was in this context that a new organization was formed in the Selva and Altos regions. In late 1989 the Alianza Campesina Independiente Emiliano Zapata (ACIEZ) emerged in Altamirano, Ocosingo, San Cristóbal, Sabanilla and Salto de Agua. In early 1992 it changed its name to ANCIEZ by adding "Nacional" to its title, claiming member organizations in six central and northern states. However, it was clearly strongest in Chiapas and had extended its base of support in just two years among Tzotzil, Tzeltal and Chol communities in the highland municipalities of El Bosque, Larrainzar, Chenalhó, Chanal, Huixtán, Oxchuc, Tila and Tumbalá. The lack of solution to the economic and agrarian demands in the Cañadas of Ocosingo contributed to the radicalization of young campesinos by the ANCIEZ and their eventual support for the armed uprising. The size of

---

19. "Xi'Nich" is the Chol word for ants. One of the leaders of the march explained how the government had tried to stamp out the Palenque demonstration but had only succeeded in disturbing an ant's nest.

this movement was revealed by the march in San Cristóbal on October 12, 1992 to commemorate five hundred years of indigenous resistance. Approximately half of the 10,000 Indians who participated were members of ANCIEZ. During the march the statue of Diego de Mazariegos, the Spanish conqueror and founder of Ciudad Real, was pulled down. Then in early 1993 ANCIEZ went underground, presumably to begin training for the armed rebellion. The clash with a federal army column in Ocosingo in May 1993 was the first clear sign of guerrilla activity, although the state government insisted that there were no guerrillas in Chiapas.

V. CONCLUSIONS

The rebellion in Chiapas is not reducible solely to local political conditions. It is a popular response to a series of rural reforms decided without the participation of representative campesino organizations. In short it is a rebellion against a new global strategy of accumulation and against *salinismo* as a political discourse. Historically, it is part of a cycle of rural rebellions which have periodically revealed the crisis of legitimation of the Mexican state. One of the letters sent by the EZLN *subcomandante* Marcos to various newspapers is a testimony to this loss of legitimacy. In response to news of the government's Amnesty Law, the *subcomandante* wrote:

> Who must ask for forgiveness and who can give it? For what must we ask forgiveness? For refusing to die of hunger?...Who must ask for forgiveness and who can give it? The President of the Republic? The secretaries of state? The senators? The deputies? The governors? The municipal presidents? The police? The federal army? The owners of banks, industry, commerce and land? The political parties? The intellectuals? Galio and Nexos? The mass media? The students? The teachers? The urban poor? The workers? The campesinos? The Indians? Those who died such useless deaths? Who must ask for forgiveness and who can give it? (*La Jornada,* 21 January 1994, p.13).

The main limits to *salinismo* were of an economic and political nature. The rural reforms were clearly subordinated to macroeconomic criteria for inserting Mexico into new global markets through a rapid restructuring of the industrial sector and unilateral trade liberalization of the agricultural sector. This strategy, institutionalized through NAFTA, was not flexible enough to incorporate the very different needs of such a heterogenous sector as Mexican farmers. Attempts to mediate the effects of this modernization strategy did not significantly alter the terms of integration for the rural population. On the contrary, the institutional reforms and programs such as Pronasol and Procampo were precisely designed to limit development alternatives to the dictates of international markets.

The meager results of all these reforms in terms of private investment contrast with the devastation of large numbers of small farmers. Even those who have found some niche in export markets face increasing debts and marketing difficulties. Under NAFTA the prospects for most of the country's 2.5 million maize farmers worsened even further. Procampo attempted a short-term solution to a long-term problem: how to reactivate the rural economy without expelling thousands and perhaps millions of campesinos from their land?

By exposing the limits to *salinismo* the EZLN has opened up the possibility for campesino organizations to create new policy alternatives. The *Zapatistas* themselves called for the repeal of all the reforms made to Article 27 of the Constitution and the formulation of policies which reflect the demands of campesinos and indigenous peoples, rather than the interests of the private sector. This general position was echoed by the Consejo Estatal de Organizaciones Indígenas y Campesinos (CEOIC), formed by 280 organizations from Chiapas in January 1994.

During the Salinas administration independent organizations criticized the philosophy behind the rural reforms, not simply their content. In particular, the reforms to Article 27 were seen as the removal of hope for the landless. The demand to exempt communally worked lands from privatization was also excluded from consideration as was the proposal that illegally held private holdings be redistributed to land petitioners. Similarly, the demand that maize, beans and other sensitive crops be excluded from NAFTA negotiations went unheeded. The last-minute side agreements to protect U.S. citrus growers and cane producers were clear concessions from the Salinas government. No such concessions were won for Mexico's grain producers.

The economic limits of *salinismo* reveal a disregard for alternative positions as articulated by campesino organizations. Although Salinas immediately adopted the discourse of *concertación*, as time passed and the imperatives of NAFTA took over, the commitment to consensus-building was replaced by a more familiar pattern of political exclusion. A key turning point in this respect were the reforms to Article 27. With its newly regained majority the PRI took less than a month to push the reforms through Congress. Even the Congreso Agrario Permanente (CAP), which includes both independent and state-oriented campesino organizations, and was established with Salinas's backing in 1989, could not significantly modify the outcome (Moguel 1992b, p.269).

The Chiapas rebellion implies the need for changes at many different levels of Mexico's social, economic and political order. But any recomposition of that order, no matter how democratic it may appear, will betray the campesinos if new rural reforms are not included in the agenda. From the above discussion, at least two broad reforms demand debate. These concern the formulation of rural development policies and democratization.

On the first point, Mexico has a great potential to develop innovative and productive sources of employment without depopulating the countryside. Many examples of democratically-managed development projects already exist. In Chiapas and other states the struggles of coffee producers have demonstrated that alternatives which redistribute income and power are possible (Moguel,

Botey and Hernández 1992; Fox 1992). Indigenous peoples have also developed environmentally sustainable projects which preserve and develop native cultures and knowledge (Toledo 1992, 1994). Yet the potential of these struggles is constrained by a development discourse which only values market profitability. It is clear that alternatives must also be viable in their market contexts. However, they can be much more than this if reforms allow for their consolidation rather than their marginalization.

In the case of Chiapas solutions to land disputes should constitute an urgent political task. Planning for regional development should also include more than simple land distribution. It must be accompanied by an increase in public investment in the areas of infrastructure, technology, technical assistance, training, marketing and pricing mechanisms: in short, the type of policies that every advanced industrialized country implemented to create modern and viable agricultural sectors. Responding to governmental inefficiencies by withdrawing state subsidies solves problems for the state but not for its former clients. Whether it is the distribution of land, credit or solidarity the problem in Chiapas and rural Mexico was not solely about resources but the way in which they were distributed. The type of institutional reform which is now called for involves the democratic participation of campesino organizations in the formulation and implementation of plans for rural development. Under NAFTA the Mexican state cannot simply revert to its earlier role as central actor in the rural economy. This is neither possible nor desirable. But it can provide the space for representative organizations of indigenous peoples and campesinos that will allow them to consolidate their projects for the economic, social and cultural revitalization of rural areas.

The creation of alternative paths to modernization necessarily entails the dissolution of political controls, which in rural Mexico have traditionally been associated with *caciquismo*. The struggle for representation and the defense of political and human rights in rural areas is widespread throughout Latin America (Fox 1990). In eastern Chiapas it is clear that the days of *caciquismo* are numbered. Yet the scenarios for political change are still unpredictable. Local elites have armed themselves to recover land and influence in the state. The ranchers' associations will not idly stand by and let federal government negotiators bargain away their traditional fiefdoms. At the same time most of the campesino and indigenous organizations in the state have expressed support for the EZLN. Caught between the two sides is the ARIC Unión de Uniones. Some of its leaders have reported cases of coerced recruitment and abuses by the EZLN in communities where the ARIC has members. The government is keen to politically isolate the EZLN and the ARIC is central to this strategy. The rebels have replied by criticizing some ARIC leaders for helping the authorities in exchange for Solidaridad funds and credit.

The peace process was further complicated by the national elections held on August 1994. The 1994 reforms to the electoral system did not satisfy the EZLN which continued to be skeptical of the PRI's commitment to holding fair elections. It also became apparent that the discussion around democracy and the country's political future went beyond Congress and the party system. One of the lessons of the EZLN rebellion is that if democratization is to advance there must be profound changes in rural power relations also. To paraphrase Pablo González Casanova (1992), the current crisis demands a transition to "*una democracia con opciones*" ("a democracy with options"). In this context some groups, such as the Frente Independiente de Pueblos Indios (FIPI), called for modifications to Article 4 of the Constitution which would include an entire chapter specifying the collective rights of indigenous peoples (Díaz Polanco 1992). A multitude of non-governmental organizations and women's groups elaborated specific demands which potentially broaden the agenda for rural democratization. Other groups demanded the removal of municipal presidents and changes in the state Penal Code. Taken together these demands could enrich the quality of representation in rural Mexico and begin to construct new alternatives and sources of hope for indigenous and rural peoples throughout Latin America. This is the broader agenda which the EZLN and its supporters in civil society began to develop during 1994.

EPILOGUE: FEBRUARY-SEPTEMBER 1994

The EZLN and the Mobilization of Civil Society

The impact of the Chiapas uprising was clearly felt at both the local and national levels. This was inevitable given the broad nature of the rebels' demands but defied the government's belief that the problems of Chiapas could be treated separately from national issues. This constituted the major political difference between the two sides when they met in late February in talks held at the Cathedral of San Cristóbal de las Casas. Although the government's Peace Commissioner, Manuel Camacho, offered solutions to concrete social demands, the larger question of national democratic reform was excluded from the agenda. When *subcomandante* Marcos recognized that there were issues which "go beyond the negotiating table of San Cristóbal", he was not giving up the quest for broader changes but demonstrating an awareness of the need to build a larger pro-democracy force in the country.

The important role played by a variety of non-governmental organizations (NGOs) during the talks helped to deepen the Zapatistas' appreciation of civil society as their most effective ally in the struggle for a peaceful solution. Civil society, then, would come to provide the bridge between the local and the national. As the rebels returned to the Selva to deliberate over the government's proposals, they sent out a clear message:"Do not leave us alone." This call took on a new urgency in the aftermath of the assassination of PRI's presidential candidate, Luis Donaldo Colosio, on March 23, which the Zapatistas interpreted as a sign that hard-liners within the government had taken the upper hand in reaction to the possibility of reforms favorable to the EZLN and the political opposition.

The mobilization of support groups such as the University students' Caravana de Caravanas and the national coalition of NGOs, Espacio Civil para la Democracia (ESPAZ), demonstrated the very clear links to be established between Chiapas and national political reform. This became even more apparent when, in mid-June, the EZLN rejected the government's proposals and instead decided to deepen the dialogue with civil society. At the time of the "no" vote most commentators focused on the possible consequences for finding a peaceful solution in Chiapas and paid less attention to the Zapatistas' call for a National Democratic Convention (CND). Little by little, however, the idea of a citizens' assembly to unite the numerous opposition movements and groups began to catch on. An organizing committee was set up and began to work intensively over the next six weeks to assure the success of the Convention.

In Chiapas, the State Assembly of the Chiapanecan People was born as a loose coalition of citizens' groups, campesino organizations, democratic union currents and NGOs. Over 60 groups were represented at its first state convention in early July. The convention supported the EZLN's call for a transitional government, a new Constituent Assembly and a new federal Constitution. The new coalition held a second convention two weeks later to prepare proposals of Chiapas delegates to the CND, scheduled to be held from August 6-9 at an ejido in Zapatista territory symbolically named Aguascalientes after the revolutionary convention of the forces of Emiliano Zapata and Pancho Villa in 1914.

Democratic conventions were held in several other states during July and delegates were elected. On August 6 over 6,000 delegates, invited intellectuals and observers descended on San Cristóbal de las Casas to begin deliberations in five mini-conventions on the need for a transitional government, the adoption of peaceful strategies to achieve democracy, an alternative national project, the organization of a new Constituent Assembly and the elaboration of a new national Constitution. With this number of people it was impossible to reach more than general agreements in support of the EZLN. The major point of debate concerned the role of electoral participation in bringing about change in Mexico. Some groups on the extreme left argued that only mass mobilization (possibly including armed insurgency) and not the elections could dislodge the PRI from power. However, the debate was constrained by the sheer number of delegates and the desire of the convention organizers to approve a common platform. As the EZLN had itself encouraged participation in the elections and in defense of the vote, the extreme left groups were at a clear disadvantage. However, in light of the reports of electoral fraud in Chiapas in the August 1994 elections, the issue will remain a point of controversy and the abstentionist position may have been strengthened.

The ensuing journey from San Cristóbal to Aguascalientes in the Selva Lacandona and the reaffirmation of unity behind the Zapatistas' demands served to demonstrate to the government and other sectors of society that the EZLN was indeed not alone, but that there now existed a political force capable of carrying the banners of democracy and justice. The EZLN displayed a great deal of political maturity by declaring that it would "step to one side" while it gave the newly constituted CND the opportunity to apply peaceful pressure for political change. In a major speech, subcomandante Marcos allayed fears of an imminent armed uprising following the national elections and instead called on the peaceful civic and popular movement "to defeat us", to make armed action unnecessary (*La Jornada,* 10 August 1994).

The victory for the PRI candidate Ernesto Zedillo in the presidential race poses new problems for achieving peace and justice in Chiapas. While many observers declared that the election day was relatively free from fraud, it was also clear that the PRI campaign benefitted disproportionately from the use of public funds and media time. Hundreds of irregularities were also reported on election day, particularly the lack of sufficient ballot papers at special voting booths, the "shaving" of voters' names from voting lists and the violation of secrecy. However, most analysts agreed that the final outcome was not significantly affected by these cases. This means that Zedillo appears to command a stronger position than that enjoyed by Salinas in 1988.

Nevertheless, there are several unknown factors which will condition the new government's response to the CND and EZLN. These include the political abilities of Zedillo himself, his relationship to the reformist and hard-line sectors of the PRI, and the perception of the need for further democratic reform. Clearly there are several areas where the PRI still maintains an unfair advantage in electoral competition and if Zedillo were to conclude that electoral reform had gone as far as it should, then he would be risking a backlash from the opposition, particularly the PRD. It should be remembered that if meaningful political participation of the opposition continues to be frustrated, then the armed option may recruit more supporters, especially among the economically disenfranchised youth. This is even more evident in the case of Chiapas. The governorship race on August 21 was won by the PRI candidate, Eduardo Robledo Rincón in the midst of widespread protests of fraud and violent clashes in Tuxtla Gutiérrez. The official result gave Robledo 50.4 per cent of the vote, compared to 34.9 per cent for Amado Avendaño Figueroa, candidate of the Partido de la Revolución Democrática (PRD), and 9.2 per cent for Cesáreo Hernández of the Partido de Acción Nacional (PAN). The PRD claimed that Avendaño had in fact won and called for civic protests to prevent Robledo from taking office in December 1994. PRD supporters could point to several disturbing incidents during the election campaign, including the head-on crash of an unlicensed trailer into Avendaño's car just three weeks before election day. Although the candidate escaped with his life, three members of his campaign term were killed in what the PRD believed to be a pre-meditated attack. The police investigation concluded that the crash was an accident and arrested the suspected driver. Following the elections another PRD leader was killed in the town of Jaltenango, near to the Guatemalan border.

PRD and PAN representatives also accused the electoral authorities of altering the voting results during the transit of the ballot papers and the documented results from the individual polling stations to the offices of the State Electoral Commission (*Proceso* 29 August 1994, p.18). The EZLN issued a strong statement condemning the fraud and called on Robledo not to assume office in order to avoid a potential "blood-bath".

These incidents and the general bias of the electoral process in Chiapas do not bode well for achieving a peaceful solution to the armed rebellion. They also occurred in a context of increasing belligerence on the part of campesino organizations which began to take the law into their own hands during the first half of 1994. Yet they may also overshadow the agrarian issue and the sectoral demands discussed below. A renewal of violence in late 1994 could quickly drag many of the relevant actors under the feet of bloody civil war. It is in the hope that this does not occur that the following considerations on the agrarian question are made. These reflections should reveal the need for political dialogue in reducing the current political polarization in the state.

The Resurgence of the Campesino Movement in Chiapas

One of the general problems which the rebellion revealed is the apparent incapacity of the government to implement the ejido reform. This is particularly evident in the area controlled by the EZLN but is also the case in other areas of Chiapas where campesino organizations took advantage of the political conjuncture to occupy privately owned lands which they had been petitioning for without success for several years. The revival of these organizations has been remarkable if we consider the level of disarticulation which prevailed prior to the Zapatista rebellion. It has also questioned the viability of legal changes which lack consensus and, for the case of Chiapas, raises doubts concerning the government's proposed Ley de Justicia Agraria.

The precise impact of ejido reform in Chiapas has been discussed from many angles. For some the land conflicts in the state are so deep-rooted and complex that it would be unfair to attribute the blame to a new law which has not yet had time to be implemented. They would add that one of the central aims of the new legal framework is precisely to provide solutions to the backlog of land petitions and to clarify internal disputes and conflicts over boundaries between ejidos and neighboring properties. According to the logic of this argument, with time, institutional efficiency and a measure of good will form all sides, these conflicts can be solved and the land tenure situation will become transparent and accepted as just.

There may be some truth to this in some parts of the country. Even in Chiapas several ejidos have turned to PROCEDE in order to clarify once and for all the rights of each individual ejidatario. According to data provided by the state delegate of RAN, by the end of June 1994 in Chiapas 78 of 2,072 ejidos and comunidades agrarias had completed the certification process. PROCEDE personnel had issued 9,601 individual land titles, 7,258 titles for individual dwelling areas (*solares urbanos*), and 1,656 certificates for use of common lands.

However, almost all of these ejidos are located in the least conflictive areas which are also the most integrated into the dominant culture and economy (Costa and Centro). For obvious reasons

PROCEDE has not advanced in the Selva Lacandona, nor in Los Altos where there is strong resistance due to a high degree of suspicion regarding the government's true objectives. In addition, we can say that the ejido reform has not had the desired effect in terms of promoting private investment. In Chiapas only one *sociedad mercantil* has been formed, and this is made up completely of private owners in the relatively developed Frailesca area. Similarly, there have been no joint ventures (*asociaciones en participación*) registered between ejidatarios and investors. It should also be noted that none of those ejidos which have completed the certification process have taken the decision to sell ejido land. In each case the overriding concern was with regularization of individual holdings within the ejido.

If the stated goals of the ejido reform are not yet in evidence, the negative impact of declaring an end to land distribution is still being felt. We noted earlier how this helped detonate the Zapatista rebellion and how it was received amid the political confrontations generated by unresolved land disputes. During 1994 the pressure for land distribution in Chiapas continued to defy the new legislation and, because of its centrality to the political crisis in the state (and, by extension, the country), revealed the need for solutions which are not contemplated in the current legal and institutional framework. The clearest illustration of this lack of acceptance of neoliberal legality is the "illegal" occupation of over 50,000 hectares of private property in almost every area of the state.

The Impact of Ejido Reform in Chiapas: Land Seizures and Campesino Rebellion

The EZLN uprising made people aware of the unequal distribution of land in Chiapas and the size of the state's backlog of unresolved land petitions. At the time that the reforms to Article 27 came into effect this *rezago agrario* included 3,483 land petitions and 164 presidential resolutions. This represented 27 per cent of the total backlog in the entire country. However, according to official figures, by the end of June 1994, 94 per cent of the *rezago agrario* in Chiapas had been resolved (*La Jornada*, 14 July 1994, p.16). Some 46 per cent of the petitions were approved, compared to 54 per cent which were rejected on the grounds of the unavailability of private land for redistribution or other impediments.

By July 1994 then, there were 989 cases still pending. These included 125 land petitions, 12 presidential resolutions, 435 petitions which had been sent to the Supreme Agrarian Tribunal for a final decision and 417 technical matters such as the drawing up of maps and documentation (SRA 1994). Although these figures paint a relatively successful picture, many campesinos complain that in fact the backlog has only been solved on paper and not in practice. Furthermore, during the first five months of 1994 those groups whose land petitions had been rejected presented 249 new claims. The difference now was that they were made in a very different context to that which prevailed in 1992 and 1993.

As mentioned above, one of the effects of the EZLN uprising was the resurgence of independent campesino movements across the state. The formation of CEOIC in late January 1994 marked the starting point of a period of campesino mobilization involving at least 8,000 land claimants belonging to eleven organizations. During the first six months of the year some 340 private farms representing over 50,000 hectares were seized. In several cases the occupations led to violent confrontations and a CEOIC leader, Mariano López, was assassinated in March in Simojovel.

Given the already tense political situation created by the Zapatista rebellion, the state government called on the leaders of CEOIC and the landowners' associations to find negotiated solutions. On April 14 the governor signed an agreement with both sides, promising to investigate case by case the claims of each group while offering not to order the eviction of those farms taken prior to that date. For their part, the CEOIC leaders agreed not to promote further land invasions. The government also offered landowners a monthly compensation of 45 new pesos (US$13) per hectare of land which they claimed as invaded. This measure obviously benefitted larger landowners. For example, a holding of 300 hectares. would be compensated for the sum of US$3,900 per month as long as the invasions persisted.

The April 14 agreement did not hold. Ranchers accused CEOIC of continuing to carry out land invasions and in early July signed a new agreement with the state governor which threatened the imminent eviction of all the land seizures in the state. The fact that the government only proceeded to evict four farms was not only a source of irritation for the ranchers' associations, but more importantly an indication of the impossibility of removing thousands of campesino families by force in a political context which called for extreme caution. At the same time, the CEOIC leaders claimed that the state government and the ranchers were responsible for breaking the April 14 accord, citing the eviction of several farms in the municipality of Teopisca in May, the arrest and imprisonment of Enrique Pérez López, a campesino leader an human rights activist in Comitán, and the failure of the government to provide solutions to the claims presented since January 1 (Interviews with three leaders of CEOIC, Tuxtla Gutiérrez, July 1994).

The main obstacle to achieving a solution is the reluctance of landowners to sell. By the end of July there were only 89 owners who had declared their willingness to sell their properties. This would benefit 2,350 campesinos with 11,910 hectares (SRA 1994). However, only eleven of these cases had been settled. In addition, there were 249 other farms (occupied by some 6,000 campesinos) where the owners were unwilling to sell. In these cases the government offered to find other areas which could be settled by the land claimants, but if relocation was rejected then they would simply be evicted. This appears to repeat the same policies which contributed to the eventual unrest in the Selva Lacandona.

The CEOIC argued, in contrast, that if the private owners were unwilling to sell then the government should use its legal right to expropriate the land for the purpose of redistribution. The modifications to Article 27 did not delete the right of the Nation to expropriate land "for the purpose of public benefit." This measure is often used to allow PEMEX to drill for oil or the Federal Electricity Company to construct a hydroelectricity dam. According to CEOIC, the campesinos, who in fact had often lost their rights to ejido land as a result of expropriation for these types of projects, should now benefit from the expropriation of holdings which they had been petitioning through the legal channels for many years (Interviews with CEOIC leaders, Ocosingo, July 1994).

The negative response of the state government to the request for expropriation was predictable. In negotiations with CEOIC representatives in June, it claimed that the argument for expropriation was unfounded since "the decision to respect private property and the will of private owners is not open to negotiation". Illustrating a central ambiguity in agrarian legislation, the government added that "the constitutional order does not allow for exceptions". It concluded that expropriation is not the only way to solve land disputes and promised to search for alternative means. By completely rejecting this option the government revealed not only a lack of political will to affect the interests of the landowners, but also a naive belief in the efficacy of other solutions such as the relocation of petitioning groups or support for productive projects in existing ejidos. The size of the problem is given by simply comparing the area which has been occupied (50,000 ha.) with the area which has been offered for sale (11,910 ha.). According to one CEOIC leader, the government set a ceiling of 20,000 ha. to solve the demand for land in Chiapas and its real objective was to begin evicting campesinos from occupied farms after the August 21 elections.

It should be noted, however, that not all members of CEOIC adopted the same position. A clear division has existed from its inception between the independent radical organizations which call for expropriation and other moderate or PRI-affiliated groups which have adopted different strategies. Among the latter, the three largest organizations are Solidaridad Campesina Magisterial (SOCAMA), the CNC and the ARIC Unión de Uniones. Each of these criticised the CIOAC, OCEZ-CNPA, Xi'Nich and other radical groups for attempting to claim leadership of CEOIC and pursuing confrontational strategies which lacked consensus.

This division became particularly apparent after April 14 during negotiations to resolve each organization's land claims. For example, SOCAMA elaborated an independent proposal which gained the government's approval in July. Under this plan, the federal and state governments would provide SOCAMA with 20 million new pesos for the purpose of obtaining a credit fund with 50 million pesos from the regional office of Banrural. This fund would be used to purchase the land which SOCAMA members were claiming and the credit would be paid back with the subsidies received from Procampo over a period to be established by each individual campesino. Part of the interest on the credit would be covered by the interest generated by the initial 20 million peso guarantee and SOCAMA would request additional support from Sedesol to make up the difference. Once the credit is paid back and the land fully paid for, the 20 million pesos would be used to support productive projects among the members. In the meantime Sedesol agreed to provide infrastructure and interest-free credit. These measures were seen as necessary to include those campesinos whose land claims had been turned down. One of SOCAMA's principal leaders, Manuel

Hernández Gómez, explained that this approach was more likely to succeed than simply polarizing the issue between expropriation or maintaining the status quo (Interview, Mexico City, July 1994). The positive response which the proposal received from the state government was seen by the radical wing of CEOIC as evidence of favoritism and an abdication of the commitment to the struggle for land in the future. SOCAMA had negotiated independently of CEOIC and, in keeping with the reformed Article 27, agreed not to press for further land distribution once current claims had been settled. In addition, the use of the Procampo subsidies to purchase land was criticized as a diversion from their intended use, namely to support basic grain production.

In the case of the CNC the strategy was less innovative and more opportunistic. While CNC groups invaded land as much as CIOAC or OCEZ-CNPA, it also accused the radical groups of politicizing CEOIC and supporting the opposition PRD candidacy for the governorship. Of the 89 properties to be purchased for redistribution, the CNC was to receive 17, compared to 46 for the CIOAC. However, the actual land area involved is not so different: 2,902 ha. for CNC and 3,565 ha. for CIOAC (SRA 1994). The CNC has therefore been able to use the strength represented by CEOIC but has participated less in its political struggles with the state government and has tended to avoid confrontations over policy reform.

Finally, ARIC-Unión de Uniones became an important part of the government's attempt to limit the radicalizing effects of the EZLN in Chiapas. Large amounts of new resources for productive projects and infrastructure have been provided since the uprising. The effectiveness of this strategy has not been entirely successful for either the government or ARIC. It appears that campesino support for EZLN has not declined as a result of new government programs, while the increasing moderation of the ARIC leadership led to a split in July 1994 as several member organizations established a parallel leadership more clearly identified with the EZLN and the goals of the CND. One of the reasons for the split was the decision of the ARIC president to accept the PRI candidacy for federal deputy in the electoral district of Ocosingo. His supporters recognized that the members should have been consulted more fully, but it is doubtful that the candidacy would have been approved.

The divisions within CEOIC may increase in the aftermath of the August 1994 elections as the new government provides financial and political incentives to isolate radical groups by rewarding more moderate or compliant organizations. We can expect the PRI to use traditional divide-and-rule tactics in its broader effort to weaken support for the EZLN and in the continuing struggle to impose the new agrarian legislation. It will attempt to gather support for a new state-level agrarian law which is clearly biased against further land redistribution. The "Law of Agrarian Justice and Promotion of Rural Development in Chiapas," which by September 1994 was awaiting approval by the state legislature, was designed as the official response to one of the Zapatistas' demands regarding the need for land reform in Chiapas. However, the draft text does not add anything substantially different to what is already contained in the federal Agrarian Law of 1992. Although, if passed, the state law would allow campesino organizations to denounce the existence of latifundio holdings and would oblige the government to investigate such cases, in reality it is highly unlikely that any latifundios would be detected due to the practice of sub-dividing estates among family members and name-lenders. At the same time, as with the federal legislation, landowners who are found to be in possession of properties exceeding the legal limits would be given the right to sell off the indicated properties within the space of one year. There is no mention of the legal right of the State to expropriate such extensions for the purpose of land distribution. Instead the focus of the government's proposal is on modernizing production and increasing efficiency.

Serious problems may therefore arise if the state-level legislation is passed. Although more moderate groups might support the new measures, there is a clear lack of consensus among a significant part of the affected population. The fact that it was drawn up hastily without proper consultation is also a source of tension. In this regard the radical wing of CEOIC proposed the re-opening of consultations with all campesino organizations in the state and that the new law should be elaborated on the basis of the proposals put forward in grassroots assemblies.

A different problem facing CEOIC is the less than complete support it enjoys among national campesino organizations which are struggling to find ways to insert themselves into the new political economy of free trade. Only a minority of these would make the issue of land tenure the articulating principle for any national mobilization for policy reform. It appears unlikely that the right to petition for land will ever be reintroduced into Article 27, particularly following the PRI's victory on August 21. One of the central tasks for the broad array of campesino movements, then, is the formulation of new proposals to deal with the social, environmental, political and economic problems generated by NAFTA and globalization. In short, there needs to be a vision for the future not a nostalgia for the past if anything is to change. The goal of the CND is precisely to articulate such a vision along peaceful and constructive lines.

It is here that campesino organizations have a positive role to play in finding solutions to the current crisis. Increasing the belligerent tone of their actions will only harden the elite opposition to reform in Chiapas and the situation could easily degenerate into armed conflict with Central American-style death-squad killings. But the first steps have to be taken by the new government leaders, Eduardo Robledo and Ernesto Zedillo. The opposition has to be shown convincing evidence of the authorities' willingness to recognize electoral fraud in Chiapas and correct the irregularities. There has to be a willingness to open up the political system and provide meaningful channels for political participation. If this does not happen many of the people who voted for Amado Avendaño (almost 350,000 according to official figures and probably many more) will rightly conclude that they have no stake in the political system and make their choices accordingly. Let us hope that the lessons of January 1 have been learned and that politics triumphs over war.

REFERENCES

Aguilar Zinser, Adolfo. 1991. "Todo en Chiapas es Centroamérica." *El Financiero* 21 October, p.56.

Ascencio Franco, Gabriel and Xochitl Leyva Solano. 1992. "Los municipios de la Selva Chiapaneca. Colonización y dinámica agropecuaria." Pp.176-241 in *Anuario de cultura e investigación 1991*. Tuxtla Gutiérrez, Chiapas: Instituto Chiapaneco de Cultura.

Bartra, Armando. 1993. "¿Subsidios para qué? Los quiebres finisexenales de la política rural." *La Jornada* del Campo, supplement of *La Jornada* 26 October, pp.5-7.

Bellinghausen, Hermann. 1992. "Xi'Nich y la cultura de la victoria." *La Jornada* 27 April, p.26.

Benjamin, Thomas. 1989. *A Rich Land, a Poor People: Politics and Society in Modern Chiapas.* Albuquerque: University of New Mexico Press.

Calva, José Luis. 1992. *Probables efectos de un Tratado de Libre Comercio en el campo.* Mexico City: Fontamara.

Cano, Arturo. 1994. "Lo más delgado del hilo: Pronasol en Chiapas." *Reforma* 23 January, pp. 3-7.

CEPAL. Comisión Económica para América Latina y el Caribe. 1982. *Economía campesina y agricultura empresarial: Tipología de agricultores del agro mexicano.* Mexico City: Siglo XXI Editores.

Cepeda Neri, Alvaro. 1992. "Chiapas: la lucha por los derechos humanos." *La Jornada* 21 April, p.5.

Coatsworth, John. 1988. "Patterns of Rural Rebellion in Latin America: Mexico in Comparative Perspective." Pp.21-62 in *Riot, Rebellion and Revolution: Rural Social Movements in Mexico,* edited by Friedrich Katz. Princeton: Princeton University Press.

Díaz Polanco, Héctor. 1992. "El Estado y los Indígenas." Pp.145-170 in *El nuevo estado mexicano*, vol. 3, edited by Centro de Investigaciones y Estudios Superiores en Antropología Social. Mexico City: Nueva Imagen.

Dichtl, Sigrid. 1987. *Cae una estrella: Desarrollo y destrucción de la Selva Lacandona.* Mexico City: Secretaría de Educación Pública.

El Financiero. Mexico City daily newspaper.

Equipo Pueblo/Instituto Maya. 1988. *"Desde Chihuahua hasta Chiapas...".* Mexico City: Equipo Pueblo.

Fernández Ortiz, Luis M. and María Tarrío García. 1983. *Ganadería y estructura agraria en Chiapas.* Mexico City: Universidad Autónoma Metropolitana. Unidad Xochimilco.

Flores Lúa, Graciela, Luisa Paré, and Sergio Sarmiento. 1988. *Las voces del campo: Movimiento campesino y política agraria, 1976-1984*. Mexico City: Instituto de Investigaciones Sociales, UNAM and Siglo XXI Editores.

Fox, Jonathan, ed. 1990. *The Challenge of Rural Democratisation: Perspectives from Latin America and the Philippines*. London: Frank Cass Publishers.

Fox, Jonathan. 1992. *The Politics of Food in Mexico: State Power and Social Mobilization*. Ithaca: Cornell University Press.

García de León, Antonio. 1985. *Resistencia y utopía*. 2 volumes. Mexico City: Era.

González Casanova, Pablo. 1992. "México: ¿hacia una democracia sin opciones?" Pp.267-290 in *El nuevo estado mexicano*, vol. 4, edited by Centro de Investigaciones y Estudios Superiores en Antropología Social. Mexico City: Nueva Imagen.

Gramsci, Antonio. 1971. *Selections from the Prison Notebooks of Antonio Gramsci*, edited by Q. Hoare and G.N. Smith. London: Lawrence and Wishart.

Harvey, Neil. 1990. "Peasant strategies and corporatism in Chiapas." Pp.183-98 in *Popular Movements and Political Change in Mexico*, edited by Joe Foweraker and Ann Craig. Boulder, Colorado: Lynne Rienner Publishers.

1992a. "Conservación a costa de la miseria." *Campo Uno*, supplement of *Uno Más Uno*. 1 and 8 June 1992.

1992b. "La Unión de Uniones de Chiapas y los retos políticos del desarrollo de base." Pp.219-232 in *Autonomía y Nuevos Sujetos Sociales en el Desarrollo Rural*, edited by Julio Moguel, Carlota Botey and Luis Hernández. Mexico City: Siglo XXI Editores and Centro de Estudios Históricos del Agrarismo en México.

1993. "The difficult transition: neoliberalism and neocorporatism in Mexico." Pp.4-26 in *Mexico: Dilemmas of Transition*, edited by Neil Harvey. London: Institute of Latin American Studies and British Academic Press and New York: St. Martin's Press.

Hernández, Luis. 1991. "Nadando con los tiburones: la experiencia de la Coordinadora Nacional de Organizaciones Cafetaleras." *Cuadernos Agrarios* 1 (Nueva Epoca): 52-75.

1994. "El café y la guerra." *La Jornada* 30 January, p.1 and p.48.

Hewitt de Alcántara, Cynthia. 1992. *Economic Restructuring and Rural Subsistence in Mexico: Maize and the Crisis of the 1980s*. Discussion Paper 31. Geneva: UNRISD.

Horizontes. 1990. *Boletín del Centro de Derechos Humanos "Fray Bartolomé de Las Casas"*. No. 2 (November),. San Cristóbal de Las Casas, Chiapas.

1991a. *Boletín del Centro de Derechos Humanos "Fray Bartolomé de Las Casas"*. No. 3 (March), San Cristóbal de Las Casas, Chiapas.

1991b. *Boletín del Centro de Derechos Humanos "Fray Bartolomé de Las Casas"*. No. 4-5 (September), San Cristóbal de Las Casas, Chiapas.

Hughes, Sally. 1994. "You Can't Eat Basketball Courts". *El Financiero International* January 24-30, p.15.

INEGI. Instituto Nacional de Estadística, Geografía e Informática. 1991. *Atlas ejidal del Estado de Chiapas. Encuesta nacional agropecuaria ejidal, 1988.* Aguascalientes: INEGI.

1992. *XI Censo general de población y vivienda, 1990.* Aguascalientes: INEGI.

INMECAFE. Instituto Mexicano del Café. 1992. *Censo cafetalero.* Mexico City: INMECAFE.

Katz, Friedrich. 1988. "Introduction: Rural Revolts in Mexico." Pp.3-17 in *Riot, Rebellion and Revolution: Rural Social Movements in Mexico,* edited by Friedrich Katz. Princeton: Princeton University Press.

Knight, Alan. 1993. "State power and political stability in Mexico" Pp.29-63 in *Mexico: Dilemmas of Transition,* edited by Neil Harvey. London: Institute of Latin American Studies and British Academic Press and New York: St. Martin's Press.

La Jornada. Mexico City daily newspaper.

Leyva Solano, Xochitl and Gabriel Ascencio Franco. 1993. "Apuntes para el estudio de la ganaderización en la Selva Lacandona." Pp.262-84 in *Anuario de Cultura e Investigación 1992.* Tuxtla Gutiérrez, Chiapas: Instituto Chiapaneco de Cultura.

McMichael, Philip and David Myhre. 1991. "Global regulation vs. the nation-state: agro-food systems and the new politics of capital." *Capital and Class* 43: 83-105.

Mestries, Francis. 1990. "Testimonios del Congreso Indígena de San Cristóbal de Las Casas. Octubre de 1974." Pp.473-89 in *Historia de la Cuestión Agraria Mexicana,* vol. 9, part 2, edited by Julio Moguel. Mexico City: Siglo XXI Editores and Centro de Estudios Históricos dcl Agrarismo cn México.

Minnesota Advocates for Human Rights. 1993. *Civilians at Risk: Military and Police Abuses in the Mexican Countryside.* New York: World Policy Institute. North America Project Special Report 6.

Moguel, Julio. 1992a. "La lucha por la apropiación de la vida social en la economía cafetalera: la experiencia de la CNOC 1990-91." Pp.98-118 in *Autonomía y Nuevos Sujetos Sociales en el Desarrollo Rural,* edited by Julio Moguel, Carlota Botey and Luis Hernández. Mexico City: Siglo XXI Editores and Centro de Estudios Históricos del Agrarismo en México.

1992b "Reforma constitucional y luchas agrarias en el marco de la transción salinista." Pp.261-75 in *Autonomía y Nuevos Sujetos Sociales en el Desarrollo Rural,* edited by Julio Moguel, Carlota Botey and Luis Hernández. Mexico City: Siglo XXI Editores and Centro de Estudios Históricos del Agrarismo en México.

1993. "Procampo y la vía campesina de desarrollo." *La Jornada* del Campo, supplement of *La Jornada* 26 October, pp.8-9.

1994 "Chiapas y el Pronasol." *La Jornada* del Campo, supplement of *La Jornada* 25 January, pp.7-8.

Moguel, Julio, Carlota Botey and Luis Hernández, eds. 1992. *Autonomía y Nuevos Sujetos Sociales en el Desarrollo Rural*. Mexico City: Siglo XXI Editores and Centro de Estudios Históricos del Agrarismo en México.

Moguel, Julio and Pilar López Sierra. 1990. "Política agraria y modernización capitalista." Pp.321-76 in *Historia de la Cuestión Agraria Mexicana,* vol. 9, part 2, edited by Julio Moguel. Mexico City: Siglo XXI Editores and Centro de Estudios Históricos del Agrarismo en México.

Morales Bermúdez, Jesús. 1992. "El Congreso Indígena de Chiapas: un testimonio." Pp.242-370 in *Anuario de cultura e investigación 1991*. Tuxtla Gutiérrez, Chiapas: Instituto Chiapaneco de Cultura.

Pontigo Sánchez, José Luis. 1985. "Dinámica social y movimientos campesinos en Simojovel y Huitiupán, Chiapas." Area of Social Sciences, Autonomous University of Chiapas, unpublished thesis in Economics.

PROCEDE. Programa de Certificación de Derechos Ejidales y Titulación de Solares Urbanos. 1993. *Documento guía*. Mexico City: Procuraduría Agraria.

Ramos Hernández, L. E. F. 1978. "La colonización campesina en la selva lacandona (análisis y perspectivas)." Instituto Politécnico Nacional, Mexico. Unpublished thesis.

Reyes Heroles, Federico. 1992. "Esa verguenza nacional." *La Jornada* 22 April, p.19.

Reyes Ramos, María Eugenia. 1992. *El reparto de tierras y la política agraria en Chiapas, 1914-1988*. Mexico City: Universidad Nacional Autónoma de México and Centro de Investigaciones Humanísticas de Mesoamérica y del Estado de Chiapas.

Robles, Rosario. 1988. "El campo y el pacto." *El Cotidiano* 23: 65-72.

Robles, Rosario and Julio Moguel. 1990. "Agricultura y proyecto neoliberal." *El Cotidiano* 34: 3-12.

Rus, Jan. Forthcoming. "The 'Comunidad Revolucionaria Institucional': the subversion of native government in highland Chiapas, 1936-1968." In *Everyday Forms of State Formation: Revolution and the Negotiation of Rule in Modern Mexico*, edited by Gilbert Joseph and Daniel Nugent. Durham, North Carolina: Duke University Press.

SARH. Secretaría de Agricultura y Recursos Hidráulicos. 1993. "Procampo: A new support program for the Mexican farm sector." Mimeo. Mexico City: SARH.

SARH-CEPAL. Secretaría de Agricultura y Recursos Hidráulicos and Comisión Económica para América Latina y el Caribe. 1992. *Primer informe nacional sobre tipología de productores del sector social*. Mexico City: Subsecretaría de Política Sectorial y Concertación/SARH, mimeo. (Forthcoming as "Productores del sector social rural en México," *Transformation of Rural Mexico, Number 1*. La Jolla, California: Center for U.S.-Mexican Studies, University of California, San Diego).

Scott, James C. 1985. *Weapons of the Weak: Everyday Forms of Peasant Resistance*. New Haven: Yale University Press.

1990. *Domination and the Arts of Resistance: Hidden Transcripts*. New Haven. Yale University Press.

SRA. Secretaría de la Reforma Agraria. 1989. "Acciones agrarias." Subdelegación de concertación agraria en zonas indígenas. Mimeo. Tuxtla Gutiérrez, Chiapas.

1994. "Programa de Abatimiento del Rezago Agrario. Estado de Chiapas" Subsecretaría de Asuntos Agrarios, Tuxtla Gutiérrez.

Taller. 1992. "Reformas al artículo 27 constitucional" Unpublished workshop proceedings. San Cristóbal de las Casas, Chiapas.

Thompson González, Roberto, Ma. del Carmen García Aguilar, and Mario M. Castillo Huerta. 1988 *Crecimiento y desarrollo económico en Chiapas, 1982-1988*. Tuxtla Gutiérrez: Universidad Autónoma de Chiapas.

Toledo, Víctor M. 1992. "Toda la Utopía: el nuevo movimiento ecológico de los indígenas y campesinos de México." Pp.33-51 in *Autonomía y Nuevos Sujetos Sociales en el Desarrollo Rural*, edited by Julio Moguel, Carlota Botey and Luis Hernández. Mexico City: Siglo XXI Editores and Centro de Estudios Históricos del Agrarismo en México.

1994. "La vía ecológico-campesina de desarrollo: una alternativa para la selva de Chiapas." *La Jornada* del Campo, supplement of *La Jornada*, 25 January, pp.4-6.

Warman, Arturo. 1994. "Chiapas hoy." *La Jornada* 16 January, pp.1-15.

Wasserstrom, Robert. 1983. *Class and Society in Central Chiapas*. Berkeley: University of California Press.

THE CHIAPAS UPRISING

by

Luis Hernández Navarro

Translated by William Rhett-Mariscal

The Explosion

From the depths of the Lacandon forest, the rebellion unleashed by the Ejército Zapatista de Liberación Nacional (EZLN) extended its range of operations into the Highland region of Chiapas, profoundly altering Mexican politics. The Chiapas uprising is neither a spontaneous indigenous revolt nor the military action of outside agitators, but rather the combined product of the work of a political-military organization and of the socioeconomic problems of the region's inhabitants. Thousands of campesinos have decided to take the path of armed struggle as a means for resolving longstanding needs and for constructing a future in which they would have a place. Clearly, they are not rebelling because they have been duped by anyone, but rather because they have chosen a path - a questionable one perhaps - in response to their perception of their dwindling prospects.

The Scene of the Social Explosion

Chiapas, as it is now well known, did not fully experience the Revolution of 1910-1917. Ironically, the landowners, descendants of the owners of the Spanish colonial land, labor, and tribute grants, were in charge of land redistribution in the state. The consequences of this situation are clear: Chiapas alone has over 30 percent of Mexico's unresolved petitions for land.

The large estates remaining after the initial period of agrarian reform provided their owners with considerable economic power from which to generate an intricate web of interests and control in regional politics. Such economic presence resulted in great influence in a state that in 1990 dedicated slightly less than 60 percent of its economic activity to agriculture. Under these conditions of concentrated power, the exploitation of land, natural resources, and labor was carried out under despotic and arbitrary practices, often at the margins of a minimal respect for human rights. Amnesty International, in their 1986 report on human rights in rural areas, and Americas Watch in a 1991 account, have widely documented the archaic and barbaric mechanisms employed in the oppression of both Indian and mestizo campesinos in the area. Estate owners, ranchers, and loggers organized their own paramilitary forces that acted with impunity against the campesinos. In contrast, the law

51

was strictly applied against the campesinos in their struggles to gain land and in their petitions for social and economic justice.

The extended webs of power of the large landowners not only resulted in class discrimination but, following regional tradition, also in widespread instances of ethnic discrimination. This extreme inequality of power appears paradoxical in a state with an indigenous population of over one million, distributed among nine ethnic groups (indeed, more, with the influx of Guatemalan refugees). The landowners' hold on power, however, did not prevent the rise of indigenous strongmen (*caciques*), equally as oppressive as the *ladino* bosses.

There were less violent responses to campesino demands for land besides direct repression. In a few cases the national government bought land from the landowners and distributed it to agricultural laborers. More often, it was decided to relocate them to the Lacandon forest. Rather than touch the interests of the great landowners from the north and center of the state, the land petitioners were sent off on an adventure to colonize the forest.

The Period of the New Uprising

Between October 1974 and October 1992 a lengthy and ongoing process of campesino-indigenous organization and struggle developed. In October 1974, an Indigenous Congress was held in San Cristóbal de las Casas in honor of the celebration of the 500th anniversary of the birth of Fray Bartolomé de las Casas, a defender of native rights. At the congress representatives of the state's four ethnic groups got together to discuss problems of land, commerce, education, and health. This exchange defined the issues and gave birth to a process of organizing that continues to this day, despite an environment marked by conflicts and repression.

On October 12, 1992 there was an impressive demonstration in the city as part of a commemoration of the 500 years of indigenous and popular resistance. Thousands of campesinos belonging to different ethnic groups took to the streets of the city and toppled and destroyed a symbol of the Spanish conquerors, the statue of Diego Mazariegos. In the eyes of some of the participating groups, this moment marked the beginning of a period where solutions to indigenous problems could only come from armed struggle.

The January 1st uprising of 1994 was thus born as much out of the conditions of oppression, misery and injustice so prevalent in the state, as from a tradition of indigenous insurrections and independent campesino struggles particularly active during the past twenty years.

Campesino Organization

After 1974, the struggles and organizing efforts of campesinos began to grow and spread. The orgins of this expansion can be traced to a variety of factors, including:

* population growth, unemployment, and pressures for land that were exacerbated in the late 1970s when large landowners began hiring between 15 to 30 thousand Guatemalan temporary workers at wages below what was typically paid to migrants from the Highland region;

* the arrival in the 1980s of nearly eighty thousand Guatemalans fleeing their country's dirty war, thus worsening the situation;

* the declining availability of virgin agricultural land in the border zone combined with the emergence of an ecological crisis provoked by an ill-conceived colonization of the fragile tropical forest;

* the pastoral activities of the Catholic Church inspired by Liberation Theology;

* the infusion of different political currents in the state with aims of promoting grassroots organizing (among others: Línea Proletaria, Unión del Pueblo, CIOAC-PCM, PST);

* and the development since 1979 of a broad democratic teachers union movement in the state since 1979 and the active role of large contingents of them as "grassroots intellectuals" (*"intellectuales orgánicos"*) in the campesino movement.

These conditions produced three main currents in campesino organizing activities embodied by the three major organizations. First, the Unión de Uniones Ejidales y Grupos Campesinos Solidarios de Chiapas (UU), established primarily in the Lacandon forest, the Northern Zone, and the Sierra Madre. This group's main activities are directed towards the struggle for campesino appropriation of the production process and their policy towards the state involves mobilization and negotiation while seeking to avoid direct confrontation. The second direction is followed by the Central Independiente de Obreros Agrícolas y Campesinos (CIOAC), which aims to organize agricultural laborers into agricultural unions on the coffee and cattle ranches in the Simojovel, Huitiupan and El Bosque municipalities, and seeks to link their struggle first with the electoral and programmatic activities of the old Communist Party and later with the Unified Socialist Party (PSUM). The third course of action is that of the communal landholders in Venustiano Carranza (later incorporated as the Organización Campesina Emiliano Zapata (OCEZ), whose main goals and activities are to struggle for land and against repression, engaging in direct confrontation with the state.

Several lesser groups and struggles also developed in the state, including: la Alianza Campesina 10 de Abril (Campesino Alliance of April 10), a group which between 1974 and 1976 engaged in mobilizations for land in the Frailesca area; the struggle against *caciquismo* in San Juan Chamula disguised as a religious conflict; the uprising of three thousand Indians armed with machetes in San Andres Larrainzar; the 27 agrarian invasions along the coast led by the Alianza Campesina Revolucionaria (Revolutionary Campesino Alliance); the struggle of the Pacto Ribereño against Pemex; and the agrarian and electoral struggles of the PST-UNTA and the PRT-CCRI, among others.

These struggles obtained different results. While some of them had their demands partially satisfied - for example, the UU - others were repressed. Many of these organizations split apart along the way, in part as a result of the diversity of interests and opinions amongst their members, and, in part as a consequence of the State's action against them.

External Agents and Organization-Building

In the face of a lack of social cohesion in Chiapas that would soften the conflict between large landowners and campesinos, four types of institutions have played important roles in the organization of campesinos. These institutions include: churches in general, but the Catholic Church in particular; the democratic teachers movement; some state and federal development agencies - particularly the Instituto Nacional Indigenista (INI); and, to a lesser extent, non-governmental organizations (NGOs).

From the 1960s on, the Catholic Church began to carry out significant pastoral activities, especially in the Diocese of San Cristóbal de las Casas. Moved by the social and economic hardships of the faithful and by the doctrine of Liberation Theology, many in its ranks became more involved in the creation of organizational spaces for reflection on Christianity. With the passage of time, these group reflections led to the formation of organizations in defense of popular interests. Unlike in other regions of the country, in Chiapas the Catholic Church did not establish Christian Base Communities. Instead, these organizations were based on the efforts of parish priests and catechists. The Catholic Church played a key role in organizing the Indigenous Congress in San Cristóbal in 1974. The church also has had an important continuing role as a protective umbrella for these groups, giving legitimacy to campesino demands for land and for the protection of human rights.

Since 1979, the emergence of a broad-based insurgency of the state's primary- and middle-school teachers demanding better wages and the democratization of their union (the Sindicato Nacional de Trabajadores de Educación [SNTE]) has made important contributions to regional social struggles. Thousands of teachers held strikes, carried out work stoppages, and marched on Mexico City, seeking resolution to their demands. Along the way they sought the support of parents, who were generally campesinos. These campesinos found in the teachers' activities a practical model for meeting their own demands. When the democratic insurgents gained control of their local, union leaders placed their influence with the state government at the disposition of the campesino movement. They made it their goal to convert teachers into campesino organizers. Out of these actions arose new organizations of differing political bents. The largest of these was the group

Solidaridad Campesino-Magisterial (Campesino-Teacher Solidarity). In 1986, a coalition formed between the Asociación Agrícola La Frailesca (Agricultural Association of the Frailesca Region) struggling for an increase in the guaranteed price for maize and the democratic teachers movement, but it was repressed and its seven principal leaders were jailed. This contrasted with similar movements in the states of Chihuahua and Nayarit, where coalitions with the same demands and tactics obtained favorable negotiated settlements. Such repression had a chilling effect on the efforts of the democratic teachers movement to help organize and protect the various campesino movements in Chiapas.

For at least the past twelve years, the federal government has promoted policies through its development agencies (especially INI, though not exclusively) which aim to mitigate the most pernicious effects of Chiapas' social disparities. These policies have consistently run into resistance from the executives of the state government, as well as from some opponents within the federal bureaucracy who distrust autonomous producers organizations. This conflict has at times reached grotesque proportions, as it did when the state government jailed three officials of INI in March, 1992 for the crime of having supported independent campesino organizations. For better or for worse, despite resistance from state officials, federal officials from INI and other agencies have played an important role in the organization of campesino groups.

Salinismo and Chiapas

In Chiapas, Carlos Salinas de Gortari first expressed his key views on rural society during his presidential campaign. Ironically, this is the state where many of his positions - by now almost completely diluted - have had the greatest trouble being accepted and implemented. If the current administration began its term by setting campesino prisoners free in Chiapas, partially resolving old land conflicts like those in Venustiano Carranza, buying lands for groups petitioning for lands, and distributing needed resources, it soon became clear that it had no political will to seriously upset entrenched political and economic interests. The governor soon found ways to set the brakes on the "modernizing" currents coming from the federal government.

Beginning in 1990 social conflicts in the state were on the rise. The state government applied heavy-handed tactics against those sectors of Chiapan society that were mobilized. Various campesino mobilizations in Marques de Comillas, Simojovel, and Palenque encountered repression in response to their demands. However, the combination of significant regional mobilization, national protests, and the protection of the Catholic Church, reversed some of these setbacks and achieved partial solutions to campesino demands. For instance, Joel Padrón, a priest from Simojovel jailed for sympathizing with the land struggles of campesinos from the CIOAC, was set free in response to the widespread protests against his jailing. Similarly, the march on Mexico City for the Peace and Human Rights of Native Peoples "Xi' Nich" succeeded in pressuring the federal government to agree to free prisoners, to carry out public works projects, and to resolve some agrarian demands. Resolution of many of these conflicts had been blocked by the state government which had been moved to intransigence by its perception that there was a strong presence of cardenistas (PRD) among the petitioners.

The Bishop of San Cristóbal's participation in these conflicts, through his support for the struggles for land and his protests against the violation of human rights, has created a major rift between the state government and the religious leader. Underlying this rift we can see the central tension in Chiapan society: defense of the interests of estate owners and ranchers versus defense of the interests of Indians and campesinos. Two events exacerbated this tension even further. The first was the intervention of the military and federal police in the towns of Mitzitón and San Isidro Ocotal at the end of March, 1993 to investigate the death of two soldiers. Thirteen Tzotzils were illegally detained and tortured. Bishop Ruiz's criticisms of these actions precipitated a strong response from the chief of the 7th military zone. The second event was the armed confrontation on May 22, 1993 in Pataté Viejo between the army and suspected guerrillas, followed by military operations in the region which led to the arbitrary imprisonment of innocent people.

Rebellion in the Lacandon Forest

Initially, colonization of the Lacandon forest was spurred by the large lumber companies exploiting its resources and by accompanying settlers seeking work. Settlement in the area later increased in response to demands in other regions for agrarian reform. Many of the settlers in the forest had been moved from other parts of Chiapas - and other states - by the agrarian bureaucracy, and others were "expelled" from large estates. The settlers that came to the forest after the 1940s because of these reasons arrived as the losers of the agrarian struggle, as people who had been unable to recover land from large landowners in a country where agrarian reform was a living myth. They had undertaken a real exodus from their places of origin, forced, as in all exoduses.

In their task of creating new communities and lives where there had not been any before, the settlers had the support of the Catholic Church. Notably absent in the forest were government institutions. Religion thus became one of the key elements binding the new communities together. The Catholic Church gained influence in the region by respecting many popular customs to form a highly syncretic religious practice. Under these conditions, catechists were key not only in transmitting the "word of God," but also in establishing links between the communities and the exterior. Literate and mobile, and many of them bilingual in Spanish, they clearly became the "grassroots intellectuals" of their congregations.

The struggle for the recognition of land rights combined with struggles for public services acted as a second cohesive factor for these communities. In 1972, President Echeverría signed a decree granting 614,321 hectares of land to 66 Lacandon families, ignoring the rights to this land held by 26 communities from other ethnic groups. It was not until 1987 that the government sought to resolve this dispute, and only in 1989 that the president issued a resolution benefiting the affected communities. During this struggle there had also been battles with the large cattle ranchers who were expelling campesinos from their lands violently and accusing them of organizing land invasions. The social identity which developed out of these confrontations was fed by a memory of constant transgressions.

In their struggle for land and public services, the campesino groups always had two distinct paths available to them. One was the path preferred by those who pushed for the creation of democratic organizations of resistance and sought campesino self-determination. The other was the path of those who thought that this type of organizing was necessary but insufficient and that only changes in the system spurred by armed action could solve their deeper problems. From the first position arose organizations like the ARIC-Unión de Uniones and from the second the EZLN of today.

For years the path of negotiated campesino self-determination had been the principal terrain of struggle in the region, despite the constant opposition to their efforts from unyielding local governments. But, since about three years ago that position began to gradually lose influence among the inhabitants of the region.

Multiple factors played into this shift. One of them was the continuing conflict with large landowners and their repressive paramilitary "white guards." Although landowner holdings were technically limited by law, the large landowners maintained effective control over the majority of pasture lands, cultivated plots, and cattle lands in the region. They monopolized local power structures and used public resources for their exclusive benefit, while blocking funds that federal programs tried to provide to the rural communities. Accustomed to quick and easy profits because of low land and labor costs - they had to invest almost nothing in their estates - the ranchers blamed the campesinos when the economic crisis hit and focused new aggressions against them. The ranchers responded particularly violently to groups petitioning for lands (jail, threats, murders). The ranchers counted on the support of local governments and different federal officials in their anti-campesino crusade. They offered "social stability" to these officials, amongst other things, in return for the government's *carte blanche*. The growing social tension in Chiapas fed on this violence and profound racial discrimination.

The pressures of Mexico's economic crisis further contributed to rising tensions. For many years four products have generated the lion's share of income in Chiapas: timber, coffee, cattle, and corn. In recent years earnings from these activities decreased dramatically. A ban on forestry exploitation decreed in 1989 closed off this activity to local inhabitants. The drop in international coffee prices (from 120-140 dollars for 100 pounds in 1989 to an average of 60-70 dollars) and the government's macroeconomic policies eliminating coffee subsidies, spurred an economic trend that eventually reduced coffee producers' incomes by 65 percent. The withdrawal of INMECAFE (the government institution charged with promoting and supporting coffee production) from the region left producers in many areas without channels for marketing or technical assistance. The drop in cattle prices also hit the region hard. The deterioration of maize yield as a result of population growth and the reduction in slash-and-burn farming cycles from 30 years to two years has limited the availability of basic foodstuffs. As misery heaped upon misery, the government's poverty alleviation program, Pronasol, could do little to relieve the effects of income reduction and lack of employment in the region.

These pressures were compounded by the national government's unwillingness to take on the tangled web of political and economic interests that generated the conflict. For years the state government in Chiapas has blocked reform initiatives proposed by the federal government. Only a few piecemeal reforms made it down to the state level, and many of those reforms assumed that the local elites would be agents for modernization. To make matters worse, the partial dismantling of government agricultural support programs created a vacuum in support services for small producers; a vacuum that is being filled to only a limited extent by democratic campesino economic organizations. Under these conditions, the organizations struggling for campesino democratic self-determination waged an uphill battle against deepening poverty.

Meanwhile, the political-military organizations that had become established in the region after years of their own disciplined and persevering labor - not the work of foreigners or outside agitators - gained enough influence to be able to unleash the rebellion. Familiar with native culture and communal practices, these groups were able to prepare militarily and ideologically with broad support within the local communities. Their movement appealed to the people's desperation with a terrible present and an uncertain future, to anger at past defeats and humiliations, and to a utopic desire of recovering a lost Indian nation.

Institutional Factors

We need to study the causes of the Zapatista armed uprising if we want to effectively resolve these conflicts. Mere condemnation of the Zapatistas' actions is of little use. To recapitulate, the uprising was caused by three basic problems: a deep struggle between the interests of estate owners and ranchers and the interests of campesino and Indian communities over the control of land and natural resources; an acute social crisis in which large sections of the population are living in extreme poverty; and a climate of violence and discrimination which has led to the interpretation of all campesino social struggles as unbearable threats to those in power. But this diagnosis of the problems, while correct, is insufficient. To our diagnosis we must also add three more elements: the actions of government agencies in charge of promoting development; the actions of the judiciary; and, the absence of democracy.

Campesinos have had few institutionalized protections against a judicial system partial towards the concerns of the power-brokers in the region. Institutions in charge of carrying out the law, and certain state laws themselves, work against Indians and campesinos. It is widely held that the police are responsible for a large number of abuses of human rights. Article 8 of the State Penal Code punishes the intellectual authors of an alleged crime and Article 135 punishes the occupation of public squares. Under the first statute, it is an easy matter to identify a person as a suspect and to jail them for months without a trial, while the second discourages protest of these actions. The national press reported an instance of a prisoner who tried to set himself on fire in protest of his treatment in the Cerro Hueco prison. Practically all democratic campesino organizations active in the state have some of their members in prison.

The lack of democracy that is stifling the whole of Mexican society is also drowning Chiapas. Voting statistics from 1991 reveal certain municipios that voted unanimously for the official party despite blatant deep internal political divisions. The Campesino-Teachers Solidarity organization's attempts at the start of Governor Patrocinio Gonzalez Garrido's to contest the control of municipal committees of the PRI in the indigenous areas led to its victories in the municipal president's races of 14 municipalities. This movement fell apart when many of its newly elected municipal presidents were accused of corruption and arrested - some justifiably, others for political revenge - and another president was murdered at the hands of a local boss. Irma Serrano's explosive campaign in August of 1991 to be a federal Senator from Chiapas generated as many sympathies as it did controversies, but was eventually weakened by electoral fraud. The Xi' Nich march achieved some of the marchers' goals except for their demand that the appointment of municipal officers be by direct vote - rather than by designation by the municipal president.

Shaking up the Institutions

The Chiapas rebellion deeply shook up Mexico's political institutions. The Secretary of the Interior was immediately removed from office and the cabinet was reshuffled in favor of moderates over hardliners. It also thrust Manuel Camacho Solis into the political spotlight upon his designation as High Commissioner for Peace. If the past three administrations have ended their terms under a cloud of economic crisis, then the end of the Salinas administration has been shaken up by the worst political crisis in the past 50 years.

The Chiapas uprising also altered the whole political spectrum. Within the Catholic Church, Monsignor Corripio removed Jerónimo Prigione, the papal envoy and government favorite, and replaced him with the chastised Bishop of San Cristóbal, Samuel Ruiz, in the political negotiations over the conflict. On the national political map, the leftist PRD party is now shifting to the center and reevaluating its legal and political chances in the coming presidential elections. And throughout civil society a broad peace movement has developed which is becoming an anti-government movement in response to the government's actions in the conflict.

The EZLN's armed uprising has provoked a deep readjustment within Chiapas' political and social forces. Although the principal actors in the peace negotiations are the Federal Government, the EZLN, and the political mediators, many economic and social groups from the state have gathered around them to express their fundamental concerns: peace, new relations of power, and resolution to a plethora of economic demands which would require a readjustment of economic priorities. While these groups push for change others push for a restoration of the status quo.

Seven social alliances have become apparent in this readjustment: (1) the traditional oligarchy (large landowners and big merchants) affiliated with the traditional corporatist institutions (such as the sectoral chambers of commerce and official workers unions) and with the political leaders in Chiapas which have yet to be "beheaded" by the insurgents (municipal presidents, local bosses, etc.); (2) the emerging local political class - especially the acting governor - and the new state development agency officials brought in to replace the officials from the previous administration as well as members of the different special commissions established to deal with the conflict; (3) the campesino-indigenous organizations in the state which have joined to form the Consejo Estatal Indígena Campesina (CEIC); (4) a group of citizens associated with organizations concerned with human rights and political freedoms; (5) churches of different denominations and in particular the Catholic Church; (6) the teachers unions organized in the SNTE; and (7), with a lower profile, the various national political parties that have been active in Chiapas.

The traditional oligarchy has taken up its typical positions. One group among them (hotel, restaurant, and land owners) demanded - and received from the Federal Government - economic compensation for the losses "suffered" by them due to the disruptions caused by the uprising, while others - the large estate ranchers - also are demanding compensation, inflating their real losses. The CNC has requested that the promised federal aid be funneled through its channels. This group endorses the actions of the military. They have proclaimed through protests in the streets of Ocosingo and San Cristóbal the necessity for increased military presence and advances against the Zapatistas, while at the same time denouncing Bishop Ruiz. Publicly, they have stated that they view the defense of human rights as an obstacle to reestablishing order. They have also accused old rivals - villagers and leaders in Oxchuc and Las Margaritas are only some examples among many - of being Zapatistas to encourage their repression. They have encouraged the non-combatant members of the communities in conflict to flee, thus preparing the land for massive counterinsurgent military action. In the Soconusco they have taken over bank offices seeking to renegotiate overdue loans. In sum, the peace that they are looking for is the peace of the grave, which would come from squashing the rebellion and would lead to the swelling of their bank accounts.

The alliance comprised of the emerging Chiapas elite and the federal officials engaged in activities responding to the rebellion is incredibly disorganized; these officials compete among themselves for their new clientele. Although it may be clear who the peace negotiators are, it is not at all clear to whom citizens must turn to have their particular grievances met: to the officials that are on their way out (because it is an election year and because of the change in governors), or to those that are on their way in? To the special commissions recently established, or to the existing commissions?

The formation of the CEIC with representation from over 280 campesino and indigenous organizations places a wide group of social and political organizations at the center of the solution to the conflict. Although many of these organizations are 'ghost' organizations in that they are not very representative, the most important campesino organizations in the state are included. For some, the CEIC offers the possibility of "civilizing" the conflict and counting with a real social class for implementing the necessary reforms. For others it represents an initiative which seeks to isolate the EZLN by "fabricating" isolated government intermediaries. Currently, despite the presence of traditional campesino organizations in its midst, the CEIC has agreed on a platform which goes far beyond the traditional economic petitions of the past and has indicated that it agrees with the EZLN's demands.

Increasingly active in Mexico, NGOs working for human rights and democracy have played an important role in Chiapas. Their ties with international monitoring groups and with the mass media made them invaluable for monitoring and documenting the human rights abuses of the Mexican Army and transmitting information to their national and international counterparts who pushed for a ceasefire accord. These organizations have become one of the principal tools for arriving at a negotiated settlement of the conflict.

For many years the different churches have been a vehicle for expressing rural unrest - especially the Catholic Church in San Cristóbal. The role they have played in "cushioning" the current conflict and searching for a negotiated settlement has been pivotal. Most of them saw the origin of the conflict in the extreme poverty, marginalization, and oppression of the native population in Chiapas. Others even put the blame on the economic policies currently in vogue. Previously attacked and chastised by the local political elite, Bishop Ruiz has now emerged as a cornerstone for a negotiated solution. His incredible moral authority among believers and non-believers alike, and his concern for the well-being and education of the people of the region, have made him the key conduit between the EZLN and government negotiators.

The state teachers movement, organized into the Locals 7 and 40 of the SNTE, has undergone internal fission during the uprising. Although its national and sectional leaders sought to convert it into a force for peace, the local union's minimal response to the events demonstrates the weakness of decisions made at the higher levels of its bureaucracy. The state leadership is split into differing positions on the future direction of the union. The rank-and-file are divided into three camps:

followers of the official leadership, a radical opposition, and a broad demobilized sector that fears that the national leadership's initiatives towards peace are a device by the national General Secretary to gain political clout in her home state. Furthermore, moments like these always bring to the fore leaders' doubts over the importance of following their personal convictions as they consider the possibility that they may be overtaken by discontented rank-and-file. Another story, then, which still needs to be examined and told - especially given their historical activism - is the current role of teachers in the areas of conflict.

There is little that can be said regarding the activities of national political parties. These parties have been undermined at the state-level and only their candidates for the presidency - and a few candidates for the federal legislature - have given them some presence and a limited voice in the current political environment.

Necessary Reforms

We must still wait and see whether the president intends to deal with this conflict by gaining time, isolating the EZLN from its national and state sympathizers, while at the same time "emptying" civilians from the war zone in order to unleash a massive military offensive. Or to the contrary, if he will initiate a process of deep reform of Mexico's political system. Certainly, an adequate solution to this conflict will have to take into account local as well as national concerns. If there is indeed a real desire to develop peace in Chiapas by resolving the problems that led to the insurrection, then it will be necessary to oppose the interests of those who push for restoration of the status quo.

We can now more clearly see what knots need to be untangled in order to stop the violence. In the first place, there needs to be an agrarian reform that would actually resolve the social crisis and would break-up the territorial power bases of the large estate owners and ranchers. Secondly, a broad plan for regional development - accompanied by a substantial flow of resources - is needed to reduce the situation of extreme poverty in the state.

These two measures must be accompanied by additional reforms. The removal of key officials in state development agencies who express solidarity with the interests of the most retrograde elements in the state and their replacement by honest and competent officials is urgent. Furthermore, there needs to be a broad institutional reform which would allow for the incorporation of campesinos and indigenous peoples -and their organizations - in the planning, execution, and review of rural development programs. Previous experiences in the state have shown that producers organizations have enough maturity for this.

A fourth point is the need for broad judicial reform in the state: a repeal of the existing Penal Code, purification of the police forces, and a reorganization of the prison system.

A fifth point is the need for a democratic reform that would incorporate native forms of government as legitimate political systems, and would take away government control over the running and review of elections. Government intervention in civil organizations representing the interest of campesinos and indigenous groups must cease. More immediately, and while local elections are being held, the political structures of the municipalities in conflict should be restructured.

Many of the reforms needed to resolve the conflict in Chiapas are also necessary for national modernization. This would be true for the need to open a path for achieving a true democratization of the country, agreed upon not only by national political parties - which must of course play an important role in the process - but also with the input of all the relevant social and political forces active in the nation. The worst possible reading of the events in Chiapas would be that the uprising stems from local causes which are not present in the rest of Mexico. Despite some efforts to isolate this conflict to only the "four municipalities" taken on January 1, 1994 by the rebels, it is evident that this is really a national problem. Without the Zapatistas'"armed criticism" of the government's policies, there could hardly have arisen the new "commitment to peace, democracy and justice" that is fueling hopes that there may actually be clean elections in Mexico. Certainly, this commitment has not been negotiated with the EZLN - just as Articles 27 and 123 of the Mexican Constitution were not negotiated with the armies of Villa and Zapata after the Revolution. But in both cases the presence of an armed campesino force has forced the government to move in this direction. The time has come to bring our political system up to date with our society. If we do not do so we will be at risk for further upheavals.

INDIGENOUS AUTONOMY AND POWER IN CHIAPAS: LESSONS FROM MOBILIZATION IN JUCHITÁN

by

Jeffrey W. Rubin

The militarization and repression that have long characterized the state of Chiapas stand in stark contrast to the vibrant local democracy that has been established in the indigenous city of Juchitán, just over the border in Oaxaca. Juchitán's democracy, brought about by the militant mobilizations of the Coalición Obrero Campesino Estudiantil del Istmo (COCEI),[1] offers a compelling alternative to Chiapas' polarized conflict. Its lessons may be particularly apt in light of the fact that Chiapas shares with Juchitán many of the attributes that have facilitated COCEI's success: political identities rooted in ethnicity and popular culture; explosive and threatening Indian uprisings; aspects of both organization and disorganization within grassroots mobilization; and political opportunities for the reshaping of power relations between regional actors and the central government.

COCEI, a radical movement of Zapotec campesinos and workers that formed in 1973, has governed Juchitán since 1989. The organization administers social welfare funds for the city of 100,000 people with widely acknowledged efficiency, celebrates and promotes indigenous language and culture, and mobilizes poor people around pressing economic issues. At the same time, and virtually without precedent among indigenous and leftist movements, the Mexican government recognizes COCEI's legitimacy and autonomy, respects the results of democratic elections, invests in municipal services, and has curbed human rights abuses.

Twenty years ago, Juchitán looked like Chiapas did until the recent armed uprising: a militant movement of poor indigenous people was labeled illegitimate and subversive, and its political mobilizations were met with violent repression, including the gunning down of supporters in the streets and the violent harassment and arrest of leaders. Ten years ago, the situation in Juchitán looked equally bleak: the army removed a democratically elected COCEI government from office, imprisoned COCEI leaders, set up military barracks across the center of the city, and stood guard on the balconies of City Hall.[2]

---

1. Coalition of Workers, Peasants, and Students of the Isthmus.

2. For an analysis of the 20th century history of Juchitán, as well as the politics of COCEI since the 1970s, see my "COCEI in Juchitán: Grassroots Radicalism and Regional History" (*Journal of Latin American Studies*, Volume 26, Part 1, February 1994). For a wide range of materials concerning the culture, history, and politics of Juchitán, see Howard Campbell, Leigh Binford, Miguel Bartolomé, and Alicia Barabas, eds., *Zapotec Struggles: Histories, Politics, and Representations from Juchitán, Oaxaca.*

Today's democracy in Juchitán is complex and conflictual. COCEI faces difficult choices concerning cooperation with the central government, conciliation with local middle class and business groups, and representation of poor Juchitecos during a period of regional economic decline. In addition, COCEI is experiencing internal conflict over hierarchical decision-making procedures, as well as over the continuing predominance of the movement's original leaders. Despite these difficulties - relatively common in situations of democratic politics - significant political and cultural rights have been secured in Juchitán and a framework for formal democratic practices and negotiation over economic issues established. In light of these striking successes and the similarities between Oaxaca and Chiapas, characteristics of grassroots activity that have been effective in Juchitán may be central to the course of the Chiapas rebellion as well.

The experiences of COCEI suggest that the strength and solidarity of a radical movement depend on the ways in which ethnic identities and cultural practices are forged into political identities. The development of identity and solidarity need not be a cohesive or homogeneous process, but it relies on intimate connections between cultural practices and political action, such as the use of indigenous language, humor, and word-play in political discourse, the incorporation of ritual activities and historical narratives in political events, the elaboration of explicit cultural projects, and the infusion of popular forms of socializing, such as the gossip of market stalls and the singing and storytelling of bars, with political debate and commentary. At the same time, the capacity of a culturally rooted movement to survive depends on the ability of its leaders to speak local languages *and* the post-1968 "political languages" of the regime, and to combine public militancy with public and private negotiations.

The long term success of mobilization also depends on a movement's ability to appear threatening and almost out of control, as well as to manipulate images of violence and indigenous explosiveness. In COCEI's case, this includes the movement's ability to balance organization and disorganization and to allow the momentum and threatening quality of disorganization to alternately surface and disappear.[3] It also includes the movement's capacity to balance programmatic goals with immersion in and respect for people's lives as they are lived.[4]

In all of these ways, COCEI's survival in Juchitán has depended on the presence of ambiguities and contradictions within radical politics, including ongoing, partial disagreements

---

(Washington: Smithsonian Institution Press, 1993).

3. Alberto Melucci describes collective action as "assum[ing] the form of networks submerged in everyday life . . . The 'movements' emerge only in limited areas, for limited phases and by means of moments of mobilization" (p. 248 of "Social Movements and the Democratization of Everyday Life" in *Civil Society and the State: New European Perspectives,* edited by J. Deane. London: Verso, 1988.) Frances Fox Piven and Richard Cloward emphasize the importance of disorganization and the threat of "getting out of control" in the successes of radical movements in *Poor People's Movements: Why They Succeed, How They Fail* (New York: Vintage Books, 1977).

4. See my "Ambiguities and Contradictions in a Radical Popular Movement" (unpublished manuscript, 1994) for discussion of COCEI's disorganization, images of violence, and relationship to daily life, as well as of the additional forms of internal tension described below.

between the views of political leaders and the experiences of ordinary Juchitecos, and between the political and cultural activities of men and women. Within COCEI, these ambiguities include the coexistence of "old left" practices of democratic centralism and male political and artistic leadership, on the one hand, and practices often associated with new social movements, such as rootedness in popular culture, respect for difference, and innovative forms of women's activism, on the other.

In a similar way, the Ejército Zapatista de Liberación Nacional (EZLN) may be best able to survive and foster changes in local and national politics if it is less homogeneous and coherent than observers may imagine. This is one interpretation of references on the part of EZLN leaders to multiple local-level leadership committees - represented in the Comité Clandestino Revolucionario Indígena (CCRI-EZLN) - and the need to go back to the villages and hamlets for discussion.[5] Dynamism and strength in the EZLN may be fostered by a combination of decisive leadership strategies, on the one hand, and internal differences and tensions that nurture and animate the movement - and at times change or weaken it - on the other.

The EZLN, like COCEI, may gain negotiating power by remaining at the border between violence and non-violence, in this case by remaining clearly or ambiguously armed. The broad, effervescent, and explicitly non-violent grassroots movements that formed over the last twenty years in Chiapas did not pose threats of disruption and explosiveness as powerful as those posed by the non-violent COCEI in Juchitán. Given the strength of old-style political and economic elites in Chiapas, and the multiplicity of ethnic groups there, it is the EZLN's *armed* uprising that has provided a threat equivalent to that of COCEI in Juchitán. It is likely that this threat of violence in Chiapas will have to be credibly maintained if the rebellion is to lead to significant reforms in the years ahead. Thus, to survive and bring change, the EZLN may need to resist precisely the sorts of efforts the government will promote in negotiations: the defining of an explicit organizational structure and the public laying down of arms.

On the other hand, COCEI has survived more effectively than many radical grassroots organizations that formed in the 1970s because it decided early on to participate in electoral politics, particularly at the municipal level. Municipal elections made explicit the question of indigenous sovereignty and government opposition, and thus served repeatedly as a rallying point for political activism. COCEI insisted from the beginning, however, and demonstrated in practice, that elections were only one part of its mobilizational strategy. As a result, its alliances with political parties were tentative and conflictual, and its ability to make broad electoral coalitions quite limited. If the EZLN faces similar options, it may benefit from entering the arena of electoral politics, but without accepting the strategies or requirements of national political parties. This would perhaps limit the possibility of rapid national transformation, but strengthen the EZLN's ability, like COCEI's, to

---

5. Interview with members of the CCRI-EZLN, *La Jornada*, February 4 and 5, 1994.

survive at a regional level, gain legitimacy, and become one of several ongoing focal points for change in Mexico.

COCEI's ability to win local support, survive repression, gain the upper hand in electoral politics, and secure intellectual and media protection at the national level also depended on its ongoing development of an explicit cultural project. Since at least the 1930s, Zapotec language, literature, and painting developed in interaction with national cultural activities, with some Juchiteco artists achieving prominence in Mexico City, while others continued their activities at the local level. In the 1960s, local students infused Zapotec artistic and intellectual projects with social and political concerns, thus laying part of the groundwork for the formation of COCEI. The movement itself promoted Zapotec language instruction, historical research, painting, poetry, and song-writing since its inception, including multifaceted projects of publication and dissemination of these cultural products in a variety of arenas. While ethnic identity and artistic activity have likely taken different pathways in Chiapas, the forging of public cultural discourses and activities linking diverse class, media, and geographic locations may strengthen and protect the EZLN and other grassroots movements.

Members of the CCRI-EZLN have also emphasized the long time frame necessary for acceptable negotiation.[6] This, too, may make space for the kinds of politics that have facilitated political transformation in Juchitán. In addition to the characteristics already described, COCEI's successes depended on the presence of moderate voices within the Institutional Revolutionary Party (PRI) in Juchitán, and on long term realignments between the central government and the local party. The movement's innovativeness and ability to survive also benefited from the presence of a variety of locations where alternative speech and action could develop in Juchitán, such as the Catholic Church, the democratic movement within the teachers union, the information networks of the central market and local media, the protected jobs of the oil workers union, and the city's Cultural Center. Both the teachers union and the Church were crucial to the flourishing of grassroots activity in Chiapas in the 1980s. However, the other oppositional locations that were important for COCEI grew out of Juchitán's urban character; the past and future experiences of the EZLN will depend in significant part on what additional spaces for voice and autonomy have been forged in its rural environment.

On numerous occasions since the 1940s, the central government withdrew support from hard-line bosses in Juchitán and supported moderate reformers within the official party, generally businesspeople and professionals. These moderates criticized corruption and called for economic and political "modernization;" some of their analyses also included critiques of inequality and calls for political organizing on the part of marginalized groups. Alliances between these reformers and the central government to subvert local bosses generally failed in Juchitán. However, the presence

---

6. Interview with members of the CCRI-EZLN, *La Jornada*, February 4, 1994.

of a moderate voice and critique meant that COCEI was consistently recognized by many supporters of the PRI as having its roots in the community and as genuinely fighting for needed change. As a result, even though most of the local middle class and elite supported the PRI, a significant proportion of those same people voted for COCEI or tacitly supported it in other ways at key moments, even if they subsequently withdrew their support.

Over time, COCEI's enduring power and the threat that it posed strengthened the hand of both local reformers and reformist central authorities, in comparison to hard-liners. This facilitated new approaches and alliances, such as central government support for moderate factions within the local PRI and the appointment of reformist members of the official party as municipal president and Oaxaca state governor in 1986. While the tension of armed conflict in Chiapas points to the need for more immediate political change than occurred in Juchitán, the role of local reformist support in bringing about COCEI government in Juchitán may provide lessons for both the EZLN and central government authorities in the years ahead. Moderate PRI voices in Chiapas, to the extent that they exist, might become more vocal, and central authorities might find in them a pathway for challenging local bosses. As in Juchitán, the appointment of moderates to positions of power at key moments might facilitate power-sharing and power-holding for the EZLN and other grassroots groups.

Pivotal national events also facilitated change in Juchitán, and these may be replicated in part by current situations. In the early 1980s, expanding conflict in Central America, along with Mexico's role in opposing U.S. military policies there, increased the cost of violent responses in Juchitán for the Mexican government. The presence of an oil pipeline and Pacific oil port and refinery near Juchitán had similar effects. These constraints did not prevent - and may even have abetted - military occupation of the city in 1983, but they contributed to the relative non-violence of that occupation and the relative respect for human rights during the same period. The pressures of NAFTA are likely to play similar roles in the Chiapas conflict. The Mexican government's desire for foreign investment, together with the international attention to human rights, working conditions, and environmental impacts that economic alliance with the U.S. has elicited, have resulted in a premium being placed on accommodation and relative non-violence. In a conflict that would have been met primarily with military and para-military force in the past, and ignored outside Chiapas, such a shift in emphasis is significant, even if it does not preclude the use of violence.

In addition, the PRI's difficulties in maintaining legitimacy in presidential elections aided COCEI and will probably aid the EZLN and those sympathetic to its goals. President Salinas' need to regain support after the 1988 debacle and to weaken the Cárdenas alliance led him to recognize the legitimacy and autonomy of established grassroots organizations, a political result unprecedented in recent Mexican history. In addition to COCEI's ongoing strength, and the new alliances that dated to 1986, this national electoral conjuncture was one of the key underpinnings of the democratization process in Juchitán. While the EZLN will likely refuse to relinquish its militancy in exchange for any particular electoral arrangement or outcome in 1994, the pressures for some sort of renewal of systemic legitimacy will probably result in a discernible political opening at the state level in Chiapas, as they did in Oaxaca in 1986 and 1989.

It may prove that COCEI's experience is of little relevance to the EZLN. More extreme responses than have occurred in Juchitán may be carried out, by the Mexican government or civil society, or both: there may be a military crackdown in Chiapas or a massive, non-violent collapse of the PRI-dominated system nationwide, in the Eastern European fashion. However, two other sets of possibilities are more likely. The first is that of a negotiated resolution, tied to the upcoming elections, that succeeds more or less in diminishing, outmaneuvering, and marginalizing the conflict in Chiapas. In this scenario, Indians in Chiapas gain some material and political benefits that matter to them, but without the likelihood of ongoing, autonomous, and threatening mobilization. The other possibility would look more like the Juchitán alternative, with the EZLN and other grassroots movements in Chiapas gaining strength and legitimacy, achieving some guarantees - for democratic rights, human rights, and economic negotiations - and becoming regional focal points of opposition power. Such regional force would maintain for the EZLN the capacity to play key political roles in a changing Mexico, and this capacity would be strengthened by COCEI's presence on the other side of the Oaxaca/Chiapas border. With or without dramatic national-level transformations this year, such a new form of regional power would indeed be a major achievement.

Acronyms

ANAGSA	National Agricultural and Livestock Insurance Company
ANCIEZ	Independent National Peasant Alliance "Emiliano Zapata"
ARIC	Rural Collective Interest Association
Banrural	National Rural Credit Bank
CAP	Permanent Agrarian Congress
CCRI	Independent Revolutionary Peasant Central
CCRI-EZLN	Revolutionary Clandestine Indigenous Committee of the EZLN
CEOIC	State Council of Indian and Peasant Organizations
CEPAL	U.N. Economic Commission for Latin America and the Caribbean
CIOAC	Independent Farmworkers and Peasants Central
CNC	National Peasant Confederation
CND	National Democratic Convention
CNOC	National Network of Coffee-Producing Organizations
COCEI	Coalition of Workers, Peasants, and Students of the Isthmus
CONAPO	National Population Council
EZLN	Zapatista National Liberation Army
ESPAZ	Civil Opening for Democracy
FIPI	Independent Front of Indian Peoples
INEGI	National Institute of Statistics, Geography, and Informatics
INI	National Indigenous Institute
INMECAFE	National Coffee Institute of Mexico
LP	Proletarian Line
NAFTA	North American Free Trade Agreement
OCEZ	Emiliano Zapata Peasant Organization
PCM	Mexican Communist Party
PECE	Pact for Economic Stability and Growth
PP	Politics of the People
PRA	Program for the Rehabilitation of Agricultural Lands
PRD	Democratic Revolutionary Party
PRI	Institutional Revolutionary Party
PRT	Revolutionary Workers Party
Procampo	Direct Rural Support Program
Pronasol	National Solidarity Program (Solidarity)
PST	Socialist Workers' Party
RAN	National Agrarian Registry
SARH	Ministry of Agriculture and Water Resources
Sedesol	Ministry of Social Development
SOCAMA	Peasant-Teacher Solidarity
SNTE	National Union of Education Workers
SRA	Ministry of Agrarian Reform
UE	Ejido Union
UNTA	National Union of Agricultural Laborers
UP	Union of the People
UU	Union of Ejido Unions and Peasant Solidarity Groups of Chiapas

ABOUT THE AUTHORS

Neil Harvey is an Assistant Professor in the Department of Government at New Mexico State University. Previously, he was a Visiting Assistant Professor of Political Science at Brown University and the University of Connecticut. He also was a Research Fellow at the Institute of Latin American Studies, University of London in 1989-92, where in 1990 he published a research paper *The New Agrarian Movement in Mexico, 1979-1990.* He is the editor of *Mexico: Dilemmas of Transition*, a book published in 1993 by the Institute of Latin American Studies, University of London, and British Academic Press. Since 1985, he has carried out extensive research in Chiapas on campesino strategies and the state.

Luis Hernández Navarro is an advisor to the *Coordinadora Nacional de Organizaciones Cafetaleras* (CNOC), a researcher at the *Centro de Estudios para el Cambio en el Campo Mexicano* (CECCAM), and a frequent contributor to the Mexico City daily newspaper *La Jornada.* He also is co-editor (with Julio Moguel and Carlota Botey) of *Autonomía y nuevos sujetos sociales en el desarrollo rural* (Mexico City: Siglo Veintiuno Editores, 1992).

Jeffrey W. Rubin is Assistant Professor of Political Science at Amherst College. During 1993-94 he was a Visiting Research Fellow at the Center for U.S.-Mexican Studies. He has written about politics in Juchitán, the internal dynamics of radical movements, the significance of everyday forms of resistance, and the role of culture and regional power in Mexican politics.

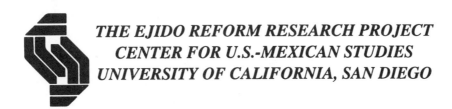

THE EJIDO REFORM RESEARCH PROJECT
CENTER FOR U.S.-MEXICAN STUDIES
UNIVERSITY OF CALIFORNIA, SAN DIEGO

In December, 1991, Article 27 of the Mexican Constitution was reformed to permit -- but not to require -- the privatization of previously inalienable, communally-controlled ejido land. The ejido reform -- in association with related constitutional amendments, revamped agrarian codes, and redesigned agricultural policies -- changes key aspects of land tenure, state-campesino relations, and establishes the framework for how rural Mexicans participate in the national and international economies.

With financial support from the Ford Foundation and from the Tinker Foundation, the Center for U.S.-Mexican Studies has assembled a multidisciplinary research team to collect key data and to produce basic interpretations that will further medium- and long-term research on the epoch-making changes now underway in the Mexican countryside. More than thirty researchers from Mexican, U.S., and Canadian research institutions are members of the project, which began in July, 1992. By combining the talents of a diverse and highly-qualified body of researchers, complemented by students training to be the next generation of much-needed agrarian scholars, the project will result in information and analysis useful to persons interested in understanding the paths of change in rural Mexico.

The series, **The Transformation of Rural Mexico**, draws on the contributions of project members, as well as of other researchers, to offer policymakers, agricultural leaders, and scholars timely information on the emerging shape of the Mexican countryside in the form of papers, short monographs and books. At the conclusion of the project, an edited volume presenting major research findings will be published.

To obtain more information about the Ejido Reform Research Project, including descriptions of available and forthcoming publications, upcoming activities, and guidelines for the project's 1995 competition for small grants supporting graduate student field research in rural Mexico, please write to: David Myhre, Coordinator, Ejido Reform Research Project, Center for U.S. Mexican Studies, U.C.-San Diego 0510, La Jolla CA 92093-0510 (FAX: 619-534-6447).

AVAILABLE TITLES

Productores del Sector Social Rural en México
  SARH-CEPAL. $15.00 Order Code: DP-01 (In Spanish)
Economic Restructuring and Rural Subsistence in Mexico: Corn and the Crisis of the 1980s
  Cynthia Hewitt de Alcántara, editor. $18.00 Order Code: DP-02
The End of Agrarian Reform in Mexico: Past Lessons, Future Prospects
  Billie R. DeWalt, Martha W. Rees, with Arthur D. Murphy. $10.00 Order Code: DP-03
Rural Reform in Mexico: The View from the Comarca Lagunera in 1993
  Raúl Salinas de Gortari and José Luis Solís González. $8.00 Order Code: DP-04
Rebellion in Chiapas: Rural Reforms, Campesino Radicalism, and the Limits to Salinismo, revised and updated
  Neil Harvey, with additional essays by Luis Hernández Navarro and Jeffrey W. Rubin. $7.00 Order Code: DP-05
Viva Zapata!: Generation, Gender, and Historical Consciousness in the Reception of Ejido Reform in Oaxaca
  Lynn Stephen. $7.00 Order Code: DP-06.